THE PRE-VOCATIONAL FRANCHISE

THE PRE-VOCATIONAL FRANCHISE:

ORGANIZING COMMUNITY–LINKED EDUCATION FOR ADULT AND WORKING LIFE

BILL LAW

National Institute for Careers
Education and Counselling
(The Hatfield Polytechnic and The Careers
Research and Advisory Centre)

Harper & Row, Publishers
London

Cambridge San Francisco
Mexico City São Paulo
New York Singapore
Philadelphia Sydney

Copyright © 1986 Bill Law
All rights reserved

First published 1986

Harper & Row Ltd
28 Tavistock Street
London WC2E 7PN

W 34419 (1) [8.95: 9.87

British Library Cataloguing in Publication Data
Law, Bill
   The pre-vocational franchise: organising
   community-linked education for adult and
   working life.
   1. Vocational education—Great Britain
   I. Title
   370.11′ 3′ 0941   LC1047.G7

ISBN 0-06-318354-4

Typeset by Mathematical Composition Setters Ltd, Salisbury, Wilts.
Printed and bound by The Bath Press, Bath

To John Storey,

Long-time advocate for the
pre-vocational franchise

CONTENTS

ACKNOWLEDGEMENTS

It would not have been possible to construct this handbook without the benefit of the development work and reports used as illustrative material. I am grateful to the teachers, careers officers, project coordinators, consultants and evaluators whose work is cited and who, in many cases, have taken time and trouble to comment on its presentation here. In addition to the acknowledgements listed in the text and references, I acknowledge help from information provided by Brinnington Community High School, Stockport, and other contacts whose information has been included anonymously.

A number of colleagues have commented usefully on the developing material. I am indebted particularly to John Storey, Northern Director of the School Curriculum Industry Project, Tony Watts, Director of the National Institute for Careers Education and Counselling, and Ian Jamieson, Lecturer in Education at the University of Bath.

Much of the material incorporated into the book has been used in in-service staff-development work. The interest, ideas and suggestions of the participants have been helpful and informative. In this respect I am grateful particularly to participants on the Learning for a Changing World projects in Essex and Hertfordshire, and on the Hatfield Polytechnic's in-service courses for guidance teachers.

I am grateful also to Jean Howell, Janet Stares, Sarah Wragg and Sue Smith, all with the National Institute for Careers Education and Counselling, for their patient help in putting together various parts of the final typescript.

Bill Law
March 1986

INTRODUCTION

Pre-vocational education is a realignment of schooling; students and society will be better served, it is argued, by the realignment of what is learned in schooling to what happens in adult working life. Too much of schooling, it is argued further, is reduced to the issuing of first-, second- or third-class tickets, which, we suppose, offer entry to working life. It puts students through a long and, at times, tedious series of hoops. At the end we know who can pass exams and who cannot. But these students know little of how to survive, cope and thrive in a working life in which they must, urgently, accept adult responsibility.

THE PRE-VOCATIONAL PROMISE

Schooling will, therefore, be less about remembering things that other people tell you, more about how to do things for yourself; less about the accumulated wisdom of the past, more about what can be made of the future; less about what we think is important 'in here', more about what they think is important 'out there'.

Curriculum has never been about the transmission of cultural inheritance solely, it has always had a prospective as well as a retrospective face. Most teachers, however academic, are interested in the use that students make of what they learn. There are specialisms that develop curriculum for anticipating the future, such as those in careers education and social and life skills. There is, then, nothing new in it, but there is new advocacy for it in technical and vocational education initiatives and in programmes in which the Certificate in Pre-Vocational Education is pursued.

The new advocates of pre-vocational education are, however, not just intending a further marginal tuning-up of curriculum; they are proposing a root-and-branch realignment of the apparatus of schooling.

CHANGING CURRICULUM

An accelerated change in curriculum is intended: more thought and action about the problems and decisions wanted of schooling to help our young men and women to solve and make. Education for performance is a design feature of the pre-vocational curriculum, emphasizing skills, capabilities and achievements relevant to working life now. More vocational relevance includes more about new technologies, and new commercial and industrial procedures, so that our young men and women will be able to function more effectively in the labour economy. The distinction between education and training is blurred.

CHANGING ASSESSMENT

That curriculum cannot be changed without unshackling schooling from the constraints of conventional examinations is understood. Changed assessment is intended: thought and action about how we are going to know what is being gained by students. Profiling and recording of achievement are design features of pre-vocational education.

CHANGING PEDAGOGY

That realigned curriculum will require realigned methods for delivery is understood. Changed pedagogy is intended: thought and action on the use that we make of teaching. Participative and experiential methods, counselling and negotiation with students are design features of pre-vocational education.

CHANGING ORGANIZATION

That little can be achieved by changing a few periods a week on students' timetables, run by one or two teachers, is understood. Re-organization is intended: thought and action on who is going to be involved in the offer of pre-vocational education. Cross-curricular teams of teachers and coordinated and coherent programmes composed of modular units are design features of pre-vocational education. So is the more extensive and purposeful use of commerce- and industry-linked experience-based programmes such as work experience.

Pre-vocational education entails an interference with the department and subject bases on which schooling has been organized traditionally. It is furthermore not to be rooted just in the rationales of its teachers and education theorists; it is to be influenced by community. That can give cause for curiosity about what kind of cultural awakening will come from an erosion of the academic base and a strengthening of coalition between the Chamber of Commerce, the Trades Council and the local education authority. The coalition is broader than that; it is supported by sources of money and credentialization, in government and certification organizations, which have their own reasons for ensuring that it sticks. The power in the idea of pre-vocational education is not so much in its novelty, but in the way in which it has developed an approach to innovation which recognizes the interdependence of curriculum, assessment, pedagogy and organization, and made all a matter of policy.

THE PRE-VOCATIONAL FRANCHISE

Everything depends on who gets the franchise. Pre-vocational education is a cross-curricular community-linked realignment of schooling to working life. It is not something that can be assigned to a corner of the timetable. It requires a coordinated and coherent use of the resources of schooling; engaging teachers, who used to think of themselves belonging to different departments, in shared activity. It also involves those teachers in partnership with members of schooling's neighbourhoods and community. The offer that is made to more people to engage themselves in the education of young men and women for their adult working lives is addressed in this book; that is the pre-vocational franchise. It is offered to people who have not previously thought of themselves as specialists in pre-vocational education, nor even as educationists. It proposes that boundaries, between specialisms, and between institution and community, are redrawn to incorporate more resources.

THE EXAMPLES

The book has been based on descriptions of community-linked activity undertaken by teachers, lecturers and careers officers. (The term 'schooling' is used to refer to the work of the education service in the 14–19 year age range.) They have sought to sharpen the application of schooling to adult working life by enfranchising more than the people who think of themselves as specialists in the field.

Some are relatively modest projects, requiring only the use of available time and resources; some are hatched entirely inside the organizations of schooling; some disturb existing structures in those organizations marginally; some realign the assumptions and structures of schooling radically; some call in outside resources and consultancy; some call in help and then reject it; some concern themselves with adult working life entirely in terms of paid employment; some look for wider conceptions of work; some generate political heat. None is included to be copied, although most can be adapted for use in other settings.

The descriptions have been developed from existing accounts, references to which are given in the text. The perspectives taken by the original reports are reflected in these accounts. The secondary use of material means that it cannot be used as evidence to support argument about what did, or should, happen in each specific case. In any event they have not been included to award graduated rounds of applause to each of the projects. Their use is illustrative. They are valid if they conjure up recognizable pictures of what we are getting ourselves into when we take the pre-vocational franchise seriously.

THIS BOOK

The book is designed as a tool. It contains things to use, by yourself, in small and large groups, as well as things to read. It will not, however, instruct you in the administration of liaison groups or work-experience programmes or parents' evenings. It poses broader questions: Who is and can be involved in community-linked education? In what roles?

With what consequences for the purposes of education? What sorts of organizational structures are being developed? With what intentions? Who influences the action? How? With what effectiveness? How are the roles of teachers and students being changed by these developments? What hinders and what helps? If you want to know how to ensure that work-experience students are not going to involve the authority in legal and financial liability, or how to book a coach for a field trip, read something else. This is less about teacher as administrator, more about teacher as manager.

WHO IS IT FOR?

This book is by no means an address to 'bosses' exclusively; the management tasks identified are tasks for all teachers. It has been designed to be used as a basis for teacher action. Its users are invited to engage in a process of critical and self-critical adaptation and development of community-linked activity.

The material will be useful to:

● individual teachers who seek community links for their own work
● working parties, teams and development committees engaged in recommending the implementations of community-linked activity
● local groups of teachers who, as part of their mutual support and professional development, want to include community-linked work on their agendas
● people in advisory, consultancy or inspectorial roles who seek resources for working with teachers on the issues
● tutors on teacher-training courses who seek workshop material on community-linked work.

It will assist such people to know:

● what kinds of community-linked activity are being developed
● what processes of adaptation, development and organization are entailed in supporting them
● where plans emerge in a situation with which they are concerned, how to make a start and in partnership with whom.

STRUCTURE OF THE BOOK

No attempt has been made to minimize the size and complexity of the tasks, but it is also recognized that time available is not infinite. The book therefore has a structure which invites the addressing of tasks by stages. There are some parts that will prove of immediate use and some a consideration of which can be postponed. These decisions will be different for different users.

In the opening chapter questions about roles and purposes are raised; such questions are basic to any task. In Chapter 2 a basis for understanding why colleague- and community-linked change may and may not occur is developed and it is closed with an invitation to spot the next thing to do in an analysis of problems for linking activity. The remaining chapters follow the analysis; different users will want to pay first attention to different parts of the sequence. The sequence begins in Chapter 3 with a look at the organizational place in which any change is to be made. It continues in Chapter 4 with a consideration of what is involved in the design of a programme of action for incorporation into a particular organization. In Chapter 5 follows an examination of what is entailed in being the person who seeks to bring about the change, the promoter. In Chapter 6 the activity of students as clients in the enterprise is considered. Finally, in Chapter 7 how community-linked activity develops in response to a variety of means for engaging people who are expected to do something different because a new action is being introduced (these include the users of the idea for action) is considered.

The reader will encounter words which are not commonplace in writing about education. Some examples appear above: promoters, clients and users. There are others; readers will be asked to cope with provisionary, consultant, mentor, mate, politico, audience, caucus, constituency and others. They are used not for the sake of inventing yet more jargon, but because community-linked activity changes existing roles; familiar words like teacher, student, parent and employer actually obscure the changes. The new words will be a source of irritation to some: in a way they are meant to be!

STRUCTURE OF CHAPTERS

Each of the chapters is set out in a sequence which is intended to be useful to group as well as to individual use. An early *activity* is designed to stimulate engagement in issues raised by the chapter. An *input* section summarizes some of the main ideas and issues connected with the chapter topic. The material is written briefly so that it can be used as handout material for group use. An *examples* section in each chapter sets out analyses of accounts given in the appendices. They are written in handout form to provide for staff-development group use as well as for individual study. An *exploration* section revisits the chapter theme with second thoughts, comprising further argument about what is being proposed. A final *action* section reviews the main ideas in the chapter and suggests a procedure to enable a decision to be made on what to do about them. Those decisions, it is argued there, must be local to the organization. The action section is written so that it can be set up as task-orientated training workshops. But it may also be incorporated into school-, college- or programme-development work.

CHAPTER 1

WHOSE PURPOSES?

In this chapter the following are examined critically:

- a method for identification of who and how people are, and might be, involved in community-linked activity
- a range of linking roles which have been developed
- examples of activity and how the roles are implemented
- a method for the planning of future activity.

All education and training are linked to the community in at least one way. A daily tide of students splashes in, ebbing with sundown, and leaving teachers in varying degrees of dampness.

The setting is an in-service course for teachers in a neighbourhood hard hit by school-leaver unemployment. One of the teachers, a physical-education specialist, is saying that every day at 3.30 p.m. thirty or forty lads (former students of the school) are found hanging around the school gates, waiting for their girl-friends. These lads are a tide which has developed a momentum of its own. A few days ago the lads caught sight of the teacher and yelled 'Sir! Can we come in and play football?'. Seizing on his hesitation they persisted, 'Come on sir, we won't do any harm, and there's nowt else to do around here'. He wanted to let them in to play, but didn't. There are no procedures and rules to cover it; it's not his job; something, or somebody, might get hurt; who would keep an eye on them?

Actually, few schools, colleges and training programmes rely on insular resources entirely. They draw on links: with parents, the careers service, Local Education Authority (LEA) advisers, school–industry liaison officers, employers, the social services, churches, the police and other institutions of education and training. More adventurously they seek inflow from trades unions, past students and people engaged in pursuit of a range of alternative social, cultural, ethnic, media, leisure, political and economic purposes.

The PE teacher is unable to report any short route to such additional resources. But on the street where the school sits there are more than 200 houses. He guesses that if, at 3.30 p.m., he and the lads had knocked on the first 100 doors they would have found at least 20 people looking at *The Young Doctors* and wishing to God there was something better to do. Of the 20, 10 would have kept an eye on the lads willingly while they kicked a ball about, maybe even coached them, maybe even set up a team, maybe, eventually, a league. In the lives of those 10 there would have been at least 10 other interests looking for a mate: fishing, pigeon-fancying, motorbike maintenance, poetry writing, political- or pressure-group activity and who knows what else? And if they would work with last year's students, why not with this year's? Who knows what between-the-generations attachments might have been made if the PE teacher could have risked 'Yes'. Colleagues on the in-service training group urge him to be careful; talk is animated with worry words: 'accident', 'no insurance', 'supervision', 'there are some funny people about', 'National Front'! The brave, or foolish, teacher says that by the next time the lads come he is going to have talked to whoever needs to be talked to to get agreement for them to come in. Other members of the group say 'Good luck!'.

That is one teacher's dilemma, but it recurs in an education service caught in a demand to adjust to the changing needs of its clientele. Flexible and creative decision making is required, but few organizational contacts or procedures exist to manage and support such decision making. Questions about the relations between teachers, students and community are raised; who can best do what? The School Curriculum Industry Project has coined the term 'adults-other-than-teachers' for parents and other community contacts who pursue significant roles in schooling. But incoming tides can be dangerous.

In the ensuing section, contacts, procedures and roles in a community-linked activity known to you are identified.

ACTIVITY

MAPPING THE SITUATION

Figure 1.1 shows a map of organizations centred on a pastoral-care committee which, currently, is considering what, if anything, the school should do to develop a format and procedure for profiling. It is part of the school's overall effort in the direction of developing pre-vocational relevance in its work. What is inside and outside the boundary of the school is located, as is what is inside and outside a 'specialist' boundary: to identify people who do and do not have some formal role in pre-vocational education. The various groups who are, or might be, involved in developing profiling are also located.

You can probably think of relevant groups in or around a school known to you which are not, but should be, represented on this map.

Mapping can be useful for its capacity to identify proximity and distance between groups, the boundaries which separate them and the links which can be made. Preferably with colleagues, consider a teacher-, assessment- or curriculum-development activity with which you are concerned currently and which, it seems to you, is ripe for some kind of community-linked change. Make a map of that activity, showing who is involved, and what organizational 'territories' they belong to. Show who and what is close to, or distant

FIGURE 1.1   Map to show development of a profiling format and procedure organizations centred on a pastoral-care committee

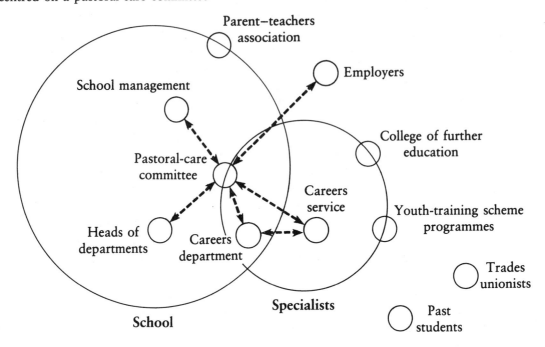

from, who and what. Show what links and shared activity there is between who and what.

- Boundary and link lines can be thickened to indicate their relative strength: strengthened boundary lines emphasizes territoriality, strengthened link lines emphasizes networking.
- Link lines can be arrowed and coded to indicate the direction and type of influence exerted in the network. Who gives and who receives advice, information, consultation, persuasion, resources, control, etc.?

With the map shown in Figure 1.1 you are invited to consider who is involved and why; to identify in what territories those purposes are developed; with what degree of separation from other purposes. Also consider who might be involved: new purposes, distilled in other territories, leading to the redefinition of boundaries and links. That would be a basis for change. But, before you make your decisions, examine the next section: it lists the variety of roles which have been developed for the variety of purposes pursued by school- and community-linked activities reported later in this book.

INPUT

LINKING ROLES

Teachers, students, parents, employers, heads and trades unionists are role descriptions.

This section lists some of the new roles in linking activity which they have been shown to achieve. But it does not use terms like teacher, student, and so on to do so.

Among the purposes and roles that can be identified are people who:

- receive benefit from the operation and are therefore in the role of *client*
- contribute resources to the operation and are therefore in the role of *provisionary*
- influence active members of the operational team and are therefore in the role of *consultant*
- design and make operational procedures and materials and are therefore in the role of *developer*
- personally deliver the resources of operation to students and are therefore in the role of *mentor*
- bring students into direct and personal learning contact with their own patch in the community and whose role is here called *mate*
- influence society at large on behalf of the operation and are therefore in the role of *politico*
- ensure that leadership and organization is available to the operation appropriately and are therefore in the role of *manager*.

Examples, by no means exhaustive of all the possibilities, follow.

CLIENT

A client is a beneficiary of the activity; a person who gains from the operation. Students are the obvious example of client, but there are other clients in any linked operation:

- parents receiving reports on their children, being invited to meetings, so that they can have a better understanding and use of what is provided by the education system
- teachers receiving time, expertise, money, plant, equipment and materials from other members of the network
- employers receiving students on work-experience placements, for the sake of the work they will do
- local people attending school, or community-based activities, as a 'recipient' or attending classes in school, on a 'return and learn' scheme.

PROVISIONARY

A provisionary is a contributor of resources to the activity, offering plant, equipment, material, money and time to the linking operation:

- parents offering ancillary help, helping with administrative work, coffee making, child minding, chauffeuring and stall minding in fund-raising activity
- employers providing 'world of work' documents, equipment and material for use in the operation's classwork
- education officials making the plant and equipment of a school available to outside groups in the evenings, weekends and during vacations

- employers making plant and equipment in the neighbourhood available for use to a work-experience scheme or to the development of community-based workshops.

CONSULTANT

A consultant influences the direction of activity, reflecting with active members of the operational team on what is happening, offering knowledge and experience to decision making and action:

- trades unionists participating in an education–industry forum, to examine ways in which curriculum is being developed
- local people participating in staff- and organization-development seminars and workshops, to give their view of the situation
- students researching and feeding back to the operation information about the needs of its clientele
- adults-other-than-teachers researching and reporting on education, and community-based provisions, and offering a directory of people, places and organizations.

DEVELOPER

A developer designs and makes the procedures and materials of the operation, working, usually with others, to put the programme of work into useable form:

- trade unionist developing materials for a classroom simulation, giving content, method and materials to teaching-and-learning pack on industrial relations
- employers sharing with teachers in developing assessment by designing, piloting, refining and training for the implementation of a system for recording student experience
- careers officers involved in curriculum development, helping to plan and coordinate the content and coverage of teaching-and-learning activities
- members of a school–community working party involved in organization development, sharing in the organization of time, people, resources and plant available in the operation.

MENTOR

A mentor delivers learning resources to students, using his or her own personality as a vehicle for putting the resources of the operation at the disposal of the students (not all mentors are salaried members of the school staff; adults-other-than-teachers are also franchised to do the work):

- local people being available to work with students on their learning, by a visit to the school, letter or telephone
- home-beat police officer being a visitor to classrooms, building up an image of the police

- employers taking part in class-based simulation, discussion, mock interviews, role play or project, on the basis of the experience, knowledge and skill of their own roles in the community
- teachers implementing a teaching-and-learning pack designed by a school–community-linked development group.

MATE

A mate brings students to his or her own patch in the community, offering them direct and personal contact with the people and places they are to learn about:

- working people receiving work-experience students, with an intention to help them learn
- local enterprise groups setting up community-based workshops for training and support of self-employment, small business and co-operative enterprise
- local pressure groups setting up community-based workshops to help people learn cultural, media, conservation, ecological or social-service activity
- parents and past students participating as individual members of a network to agree to meet students away from school to present their own roles and activity as members of adult working life in the community.

POLITICO

A politico influences society at large on behalf of the operation and its clientele, canvassing, promoting, disseminating, negotiating and persuading others to take attitudes and decisions in its favour (the assumption is not so much that students need to learn and change, more that it is society which needs to learn and change):

- members of school–community forum feeding back information and argument to higher levels in the decision-making chain, canvassing for more resources and support
- teachers engaging in public relations and dissemination work, to make the operation visible and to make its value manifest inside the system, in the neighbourhood and in the media
- trades unionists compaigning on behalf of the people the network operation exists to help
- education officials linking to other organizations and networks, in the neighbourhood and beyond, to coordinate 'local authority' as a counterpoise to 'centrist clout'.

MANAGER

A manager ensures that leadership and organization are available to develop the intentions of the operation, to resource it, to co-ordinate its activities into a coherent, recognizable and valued whole, to handle conflicts and to ensure that it reaches its goals efficiently. Different managers combine the leadership and organization elements of their role in different proportions. Different managers offer different acknowledgement to other people's management roles. Senior staff are not the only managers:

- adults-other-than-teachers promoting ideas for new activity; canvassing reactions from people who might be involved; providing opportunities for sharpening and refining the ideas as a basis for action
- school management identifying people, places and materials which are required; motivating commitment; organizing the links and boundaries required for co-ordinated activity
- advisory staff monitoring involvements, identifying dissatisfactions; providing opportunities for the resolution of conflicts; supporting involvement
- teachers monitoring activity; arranging for evaluation; ensuring that useable information is given to participants.

EXAMPLES

IDEAS FOR ACTION

Simplified maps and short accounts of community-linked activity follow. These are chosen for their diversity and are examples of what can be done. These and other examples in this book are set out in Table 1.1.

Table 1.1   Examples of community-linked activity and roles

Activity	Client	Provisionary	Consultant	Developer	Mentor	Mate	Politico	Manager
			Roles described for adults-other-than-teachers					
Department based	D3	A7 D3	A1	A1	A7 D3	A1 D3		
Institution based	A6 B2 D2	A2 A6 B2	A2 B1 B2	A2 A6 B2	A6 B2	A2 A6 B2 C2 D1	A6 B2	
Share based	A3	A3 A4 F2	A3 A4 F2	A4 F2	A3 A4 F2	A3 A4 F2	F2	A3
Community based	A5 C3	A5 C1	A5 C1 C3 F1	A5	A5	A5 C1 C3	A5 C1 F1	A5 C1

Some activities are organized from within a department, faculty or, in some cases, subject and are termed collectively *department based*. Others are organized wholly from inside the institution, but involve the cooperation of a number of departments. These are termed *institution based*. In some the operation shares organization with partners, usually by setting up a steering group or working party in which members of the school and representatives of other organizations are members. These operations are termed *share based*. In some cases the operation is run on the basis of an organizational structure based outside the school, college or training programme. A school, along with other schools, colleges and training programmes, would be part of a separate organization and are termed *community based*.

The examples are set out to analyse the variety of roles performed by different members of each network. In some cases the roles that can be achieved by people who are not officials or professionals within the education system are very limited. In other cases more influential roles are accessible to them. In the tabulation the roles accessible to such adults-other-than-teachers are shown for each example. The term adults-other-than-teachers is used here, however, to include students.

Other chapters contain additional accounts of school- and community-linked activity and these have also been entered in Table 1.1. You will find examples coded: B in Chapter 2: C in Chapter 3; D in Chapter 5; F in Chapter 7.

A1 Work Shadowing at Crofton School

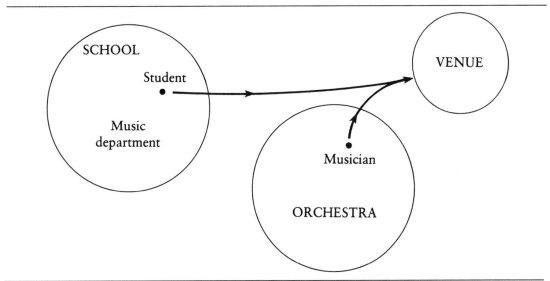

The concern is to offer members of the school orchestra a day-long contact with members of a professional symphony orchestra during their journey to, rehearsals for and participation in a performance. Objectives are not defined more precisely than that; reliance is placed upon the experience to speak for itself, in a way which will be different for each student. The event is organized by the music department and is part of its established industry-linked activity.

Client	The event is designed to help members of the school orchestra.
Provisionary	Time is found from the rehearsal programme for the school orchestra. The goodwill of the professional orchestra is essential.
Consultant	The local Industry Project Co-ordinator assists the teacher in making the initial contact. The orchestra's Chief Executive becomes active in the development of the project; briefing his own people on the need for friendly initiative with the students; later developing the idea that students live for a day or two with musicians — so that they can gain more insight into lifestyle.
Developer	
Mentor	Members of the orchestra assist the music teacher with preparatory talks in the run-up to the day. The music teacher reviews the day with students, using an evaluation questionnaire. There are plans to bring members of the orchestra to run music workshops in the school.
Mate	Musicians link with students during the journey, invite students to sit with them during rehearsals and become individual focuses for attention by students during the performance.
Politico	A note is put in the concert programme explaining the project.
Manager	The organization is wholly music-department based. The event is not precisely planned, relying on friendliness, informality and self-selection between students and musicians.

Source: Watts, 1986.

A2 The Parkway Project and City-as-school

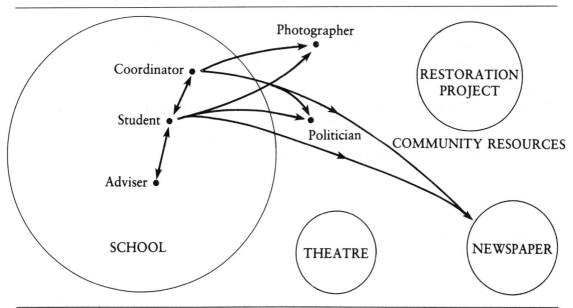

The concern is to provide direct and personal contact with the people and places to be learned about. Students select a series of 9-week placements and spend 4 days of each school week on them. The placements cover the whole school curriculum (City-as-school). Students are helped to select placements by advisors based in schools; advisors also help them review their learning. Community resources are identified by school-based coordinators, who help people there to develop teaching-and-learning methods.

Client	All school students participate in the scheme. Community resource people get 'free labour', as an acknowledged part of 'the deal'.
Provisionary	Community contacts donate free-rent accommodation for classroom work (Parkway). The project requires the setting aside of workers' time by their managers.
Consultant	Coordinators assist community-resource people in developing teaching-and-learning programmes and monitor them for quality.
Developer	Coordinators identify and recruit resources and prepare directory for use by students. Community-resource people develop experience-based teaching-and-learning programmes.
Mentor	Coordinators and advisors plan and review placements with students; tutor them in completing written assignments. Formal classroom teaching is kept to a minimum. Students gain high-school credits from their assignments.

Mate	The operation is dependent on the provision and effectiveness of community resources and the people who run the teaching-and-learning programmes there.
Politico	The original arguments are for cost effectiveness and improved teacher–student ratios (Parkway). Coordinators 'finesse' their way into finding and negotiating outside help. Tensions with the district administration and teacher unions are handled by school staff.
Manager	School head delegates to coordinators and advisers all day-to-day management, but policy is achieved through a management group which he leads. The school programme is dependent on community placements and its work must be planned around their availability (City-as-school).

Source: Law, 1982.

A3   Transition to Working Life Project

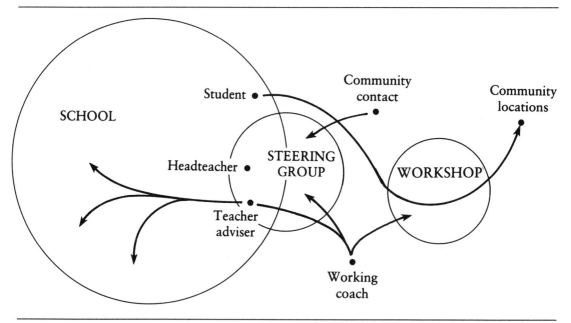

The concern is to put students into contact with 'ordinary people' — working coaches — from adult and working life in the community. This is done in weekly workshops held off school premises. A steering group comprising school and community members is established across the boundary of the school. The steering group considers the operation of the workshops. It also considers implications for curriculum. The school does not control the workshops. The overall design of the project has been developed and piloted by the Grubb Institute.

Client	Students — usually 16–18-year-olds — self-select into workshops, six to ten in each, on the basis of their own sense of being in transition from schooling to working life. Joining the group is a personal decision.

Provisionary	Employers release members of their workforces to act as working coaches in workshops.
Consultant	Students influence the development of workshops. They progressively take the lead. All members of the steering group consider and reflect upon the operation of the workshop and on the implications of what is learned there for curriculum. A teacher adviser has weekly consultations with the working coach. Commonly there is — at community and district level — consultative help available from somebody who has an understanding of the Grubb Institute's thinking and methods.
Developer	The working coach accepts responsibility for the phasing, content and development of the workshops.
Mentor	The working coach — a non-authoritarian person — runs the workshops, but not in any formal sense as 'teacher'. The workshops focus on the experience of students and the working coach. Handling conflict between members is an important part of the work. Other community contacts are brought in for visits where it is agreed they can help — e.g. with 'being interviewed for a job' or 'getting on with authority figures'.
Mate	In addition to running the workshops the working coach arranges for visits to other community learning locations — such as the law courts or local firms.
Politico	It is a design feature that no caucus swamps the steering group with its influence.
Manager	Management is vested in steering group under the chairmanship of school head, but comprising school and community representations.

Sources: Grubb Institute of Behavioural Studies, 1982; TWL Network Resources Centre, 1982; Reed and Bazalgette, 1983; Armstrong *et al.*, 1984.

A4   The Industry Project in Cleveland

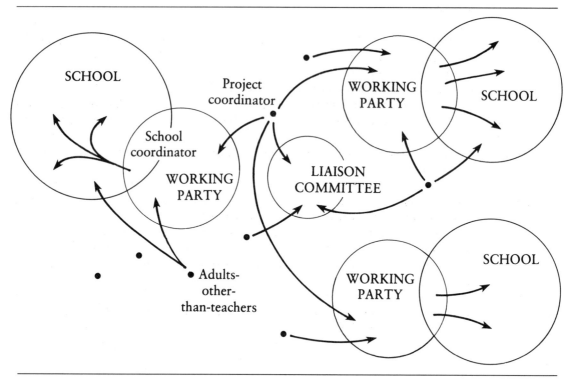

The concern is to get the realities of industry and commerce represented in the curriculum of schools. A central School Curriculum Industry Project team supports a network of project coordinators in local education authorities. The project does not script the action in schools — 'no prescription, no package'. Operational procedures are different in each location. In Cleveland each project school has a school coordinator and a community-linked working party. Working parties are curriculum-review groups, developing and delivering various aspects of the school curriculum. There is also an authority-wide liaison committee supported largely by trade-union interests, offering contacts to working parties.

Client	Students on any course which becomes a focus for working-party activity gain from the project. Parents and others receive plain-language explanations of how the projects' activities operate.
Provisionary	Working party members provide 'world of work' materials and equipment for use in teaching-and-learning work in schools. LEA and the Industry Project share funding of project coordinators. Local firms make the time of their employees available to the project. The project coordinator has established a resource centre of locally generated materials for use by local schools.
Consultant	Working parties are curriculum-review groups, in-service training groups and producers of background information for guides and directories of contacts. School coordinators survey and support involvement by colleagues. After 2 years a liaison

committee is established by the project coordinator and local trades unionists, to support working parties seeking further contacts — particularly on issues of conflict and negotiation in working life. The central team run consultative, training, exchange and dissemination events for project coordinators.

Developer	Working parties are also syllabus-development groups; development includes teaching-and-learning packs — such as the 'Lego Game' a production-line simulation developed by a trade unionist — and directories of resources available to the schools and their students.
Mentor	'Adults-other-than-teachers' come into schools as participants in 'lessons', advisers in young-enterprise schemes, for 'mock interviews', etc. Existing teacher–student relations are influenced by these developments; the use of participative and experiential methods has increased.
Mate	Adults-other-than-teachers receive work-experience students. The experience base is extended, e.g. to conservation projects. The idea is mooted to establish a cooperative for students to run with the help of adults-other-than-teachers.
Politico	Project coordinators canvass, through meetings, leaflets, press releases, etc., for involvement in school and community. The central team represents the ideology and practice of the project nationally, through the media, publication, conferences, etc.
Manager	Project coordinators and school coordinators catalyse and identify possible developments. Management of school resources is handled by school management. Originally the project operated one working party for several schools; now each school has its own working party. The working party provides structure and requires accountability for community-linked work in each school.

Source: Holmes and Lightfoot, 1981; Marsh, 1981, 1982; Jamieson and Lightfoot, 1982; Holmes and Jamieson, 1983; Watts, 1983.

A5   Post-Youth Training Scheme Partnerships

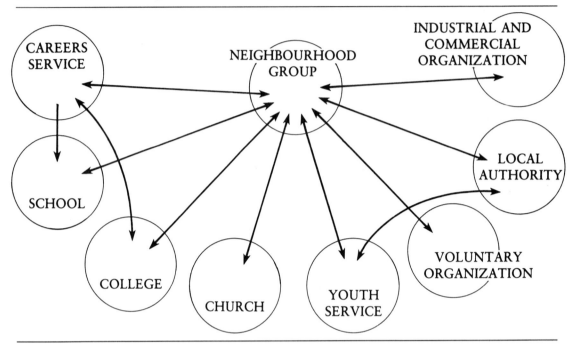

The concern is to identify and respond to the needs of young trainees, who — having completed their training — have no jobs to go to. The neighbourhood partnership enquires into need and available resources, makes the contribution of each resource visible to the whole network, makes the whole visible to local people, consults local people and seeks to influence policy makers.

Client	People in touch with constituent organizations can gain from work represented in the constituent organization.
Provisionary	Industrial and commercial organizations and local authorities donate space, plant, equipment and money for the development of workshops and curriculum. Schools and colleges make space available — for example, as drop-in centres. Fee concessions are offered to unwaged people. Government funding is sought for neighbourhood-based workers.
Consultant	Members compare, cross-fertilize and coordinate action. Local people are consulted on the use they are able to make of provisions.
Developer	Members develop advertising and information, e.g. booklets on the whole range of provisions to local people.
Mentor	School and college staff are informed on changing conditions locally. Contacts are made with people who are 'franchised' as teachers on courses. Courses are constructed by colleges to respond to changing needs — focusing on new skills, new forms of work and welfare rights.

Mate	Local people help to run a variety of conventions, conferences, workshops and projects available in different parts of the network — outside the formal education system. Careers officers are assigned to detached roles on the clients' 'turf'.
Politico	Members assemble information with which to argue with decision makers higher in the decision-making chain, for example in extending the range and duration of funding for courses, and in arguing for job creation in the area. Links are established with other groups — at neighbourhood and wider levels. Campaigns are mounted on behalf of the group's clientele. The partnership counterpoises 'centrist clout' with 'local authority'.
Manager	The partnership maximizes the value and accessibility of provision, minimizes duplication and cross-fertilizes experience. Leadership and focus for organization for activity is difficult to identify. It requires one or more of the constituents to get things started and supported. It will be different in different areas.

Source: Tucker, 1985. (Note: This is a collection of reports gained from a national survey and used as a basis for a proposal for local coordinating groups.)

A6   Brinnington Community High School

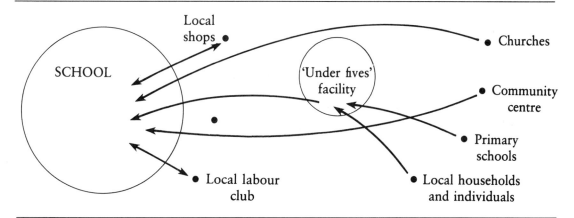

The concern is to make the personal and physical resources of the school available to the use of a community which has proven its interest in the school by campaigning for its survival and in which high levels of unemployment are leaving people with restricted opportunity for active and companionable lives, or — as the school prefers to put it — 'more opportunities for the use of increased leisure time'.

Client	Local people attend day and evening classes in a variety of cultural and leisure activities. Plain-language information is put out in a series of newsletters. Any member of the community can participate.

Provisionary	Teachers work day and evening community sessions. They are not always paid for this. Community contacts are recruited to help with school activities — such as reorganizing the school library. Participants pay weekly subscriptions when they attend. The LEA funds a community coordinator. Its initial policy of 'nil cost' has not proved viable. Crèche facilities are provided. Sports facilities of the school are open to community use.
Consultant	Staff are initially consulted about possibilities in a 2-day in-service event incorporating visits to other community schools. Members of the community are consulted through advertising material which appeals for suggestions and help and through a local survey of opinion.
Developer	A regular newsletter goes out half-termly to all the school's contacts in the community. There is also a stream of attractive, and often amusing, leaflets and posters. Members of the community design some activities.
Mentor	Sessions include classes and local events. Some initial unease is expressed by teachers concerning having adults in day-time classes. Some 'additional' classes are run now by members of the community.
Mate	Local people help with the school's work experience and voluntary-work programmes.
Politico	The school was saved from closure in part by local political action. The school has significant support on the local council. It maintains close liaison with and canvasses support from local shops, the community centre, etc.
Manager	Initial leadership is given by the school head. A community coordinator is appointed to provide day-to-day leadership, to organize the events, expand the links and ensure the community can use them.

Source: Used with permission of Brinnington Community High School, Brinnington, Stockport.

A7 The Working Lives Project

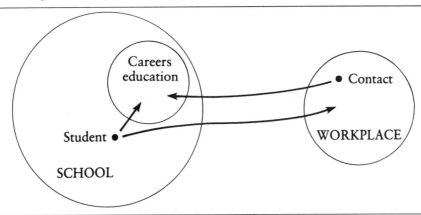

The concern is to use available timetable (2 × 45 min a week) to provide opportunities for direct and personal contact between students and representatives of adult and working life in the neighbourhood. A project for a TV-style production is established over a term. It involves task teams of students doing the design, production, enquiry, technical, graphical, negotiating and communicating work. Each unit in the production has at least three periods of plenary classtime: to rehearse, to 'shoot' the studio session and to review its impact. Other classtime is given to detailed task–group work. Contacts with adults-other-than-teachers is made in classtime and out-of-class in voluntary time. Originally concentrating on work in employment, later developments of the project produce material on wider concepts of work and alternative lifestyles.

Client	The package is intended as a skill-, knowledge- and concept-development experience for students on a careers-education course. Students are sufficiently motivated to do out-of-class work.
Provisionary	The programme can be run with routinely available resources and some goodwill. Employers are asked to release people for a few hours of contact with students.
Consultant	The students consult with each other on what they already know, on the range, sample and content of their enquiries and the methods to be employed. The teacher is the students' consultant. He encourages the students to formulate questions which will reach the personal experience and feelings of contacts. He reviews with them what they are learning.
Developer	Students form teams for each unit in the package. Students do all the detailed work on finding and presenting information and impressions. The resulting package is reusable in the school. It has five units — on nursing, police work, tool making, teaching and library work.
Mentor	Community contacts visit schools in classtime to participate in production of studio-simulated sequences — drawing on their natural authority as members of various aspects of adult and working life in the neighbourhood. They have been briefed in advance — by the students — concerning what they will be asked about.

Mate	Some of the back-up work is carried out on employer's premises — mainly negotiating with contacts and getting location pictures.
Politico	Students are asked to show their work to council members; they use the opportunity to speak of the value of this style of work, much of which is in meeting people 'who know what work is really like'.
Manager	The teacher promotes the idea to students and suggests key features. The teacher is resource coordinator to the project. He also consults with students on its scope, contacts and methods, and on the establishment of a running order and deadlines for each phase of work.

Source: Law and Storey, 1986. (Note: the original project used tape–slide techniques; it antedates the availability of videorecording.)

EXPLORATION

SECOND THOUGHTS ON FRANCHISING

CHANGING ROLES

When parents come into school or college there is a shared and more-or-less stable expectation about how they will or, at least, should behave. To greater and lesser extents such expectations are also shared with careers officers, business managers, trades unionists and students about how they behave in school. Some people think they know how teachers should behave. Similarities between the behaviour of people in the same position permit us to use the word role.

With its origins in the theatre, the word expresses the idea of a script attached to a social position. It encourages us to expect that this role-occupant's behaviour will be similar to that of other people occupying the same position and therefore, to some extent, will be predictable. Roles are defined at all levels of generality: men and women, as well as husband, breadwinner and mother, have been scripted in that way.

Franchising rewrites social scripts and that is disturbing. In the development of a Community Contacts Directory, described later in this book (C2), parents are surprised and disturbed by the suggestion that they should act as consultants to students, asking 'why are the teachers asking us to do this kind of work, this is their job?'. It is not part of a parent's script to help with the education of other people's children.

USERS, PROMOTORS AND AUDIENCES

Writings about change in schooling have produced new role terms, which cut across distinctions between parent, student, teacher, business manager and trades unionist. For example, users are people who are expected to do something different as a consequence of innovation. It is often assumed that the users are teachers, but in City-as-school (A2) users are also community-resource people: business managers, trades unionists, journalists, politicians and past students. In work shadowing at Crofton School (**A1**) the users are members of a symphony orchestra.

The term promoters refers to people who seek to get new ideas adopted. They are not necessarily bosses or curriculum developers in central positions; indeed much of the argument is for users promoting their own ideas. In the Working Lives Project (**A7**) it is a teacher who first puts forward the curriculum idea. In the Industry Project (**A4**) and the Transition to Working Life Project (**A3**) catalysing action is shared between central and grass-rooted people. It is, for example, undertaken by people like the trades unionist in Cleveland who designs and promotes the production-line simulation.

The term audiences is used to refer to people who are not involved in the action directly, but who have an interest in its progress. Parents may be audiences in this sense, so may politicians or colleagues eleswhere in the organization. In the Post-Youth Training Scheme Partnerships (**A5**), the Industry Project and work shadowing at Crofton School there are explicit concerns with useful presentation of the innovation to such audiences.

GUESTS AND HOSTS

Another piece of coinage is the Industry Project's adults-other-than-teachers: people who are not formal members of the organization of schooling or its professions, but whose educative role is franchised by that system.

The analysis of roles given previously in this chapter elaborates that concept. It is also based on another, more general, distinction: between guests and hosts. Many organizations incorporate such a distinction, certainly families and hotels, but there are recognizable parallels in other organizations, such as hospitals, schools and colleges.

Hosts are expected to be familiar with the place, its procedures and people, it is their territory, they move comfortably about it, they control what is provided and are gatekeepers on who goes where. Nobody is surprised if they resist intrusion on what they take to be reserved territory. Guests are expected to receive what is provided, their acknowledgement of what they are receiving may be expressed in the form of a gift, but it gives them no right to expect to initiate departures from established practice. In a guest–host relation there is an expectation of best behaviour; where relaxation occurs it becomes increasingly difficult to tell who is guest and who is host.

In schooling most teachers are in the role of hosts and most parents are in the role of guests. Outside consultants have been reported also to be in the role of guests: people to be made welcome and helped to do their job, but not people to be involved integrally in mainstream action. The problem of gaining entry, realigning their role as consultant-to-client, rather than guest-to-host, is reported as a problem for such outsiders (Evans and Law, 1984).

CLIENT, PROVISIONARY, CONSULTANT, DEVELOPER AND MANAGER

Once a general alignment, like that between women and men, is disturbed, then scripts for associated roles, such as mother and breadwinner, will also be disturbed. The realignment of who is guest and who is host also has its concomitants.

Teachers become consultants, people to whom others turn for help in the working up of a curriculum which, then, becomes joint property. In City-as-school (**A2**) and the Transition to Working Life Project (**A3**) teachers work with adults-other-than-teachers to help them develop work with students.

Teachers become clients. There are times in the Industry Project in Cleveland (**A4**) when teachers are dependent for professional-level advice and help from adults-other-than-teachers, and that, reciprocally, casts adults-other-than-teachers in the role of consultants.

Adults-other-than-teachers become provisionaries, not just in the sense of gifting marginal money or offering to drive the minibus, but as a major component in the mainstream planning of resources. The head of City-as-school reports that a major part of planning of curriculum must be related to community resources being offered at the time.

Adults-other-than-teachers and students become developers of the artifacts of schooling. Post-Youth Training Scheme Partnerships (**A5**) rely heavily on the capacity of all sections of the network to produce and present material for client groups effectively. In the Working Lives Project (**A7**) the materials which represent curriculum content are made by the students.

Adults-other-than-teachers become hosts. The working coach in the Transition to Working Life Project hosts his or her own territory, so do community-resource people working with the Parkway Project (**A2**) and members of the symphony orchestra with students from Crofton School.

Teachers and adults-other-than-teachers become managers. They organize the development of intentions and the availability of resources in a way which is both useable and valuable to client groups. The Working Lives Project is a teaching-and-learning strategy based on the skills of managing resources.

MENTOR, MATE AND POLITICO

Changes in sex—role relations are accompanied by changes in the usage of words. The words are important. New usages, such as partner and spouse, become more common because they represent the reality more accurately and are free of unwanted connotations. Some of the traditional role descriptors in schooling, such as teacher, may, in the context of the pre-vocational franchise, prove as misleading and badly connoted. New terms such as mentor, mate and politico are suggested, not merely to irritate opponents of jargon, but to reflect (and to provoke) new thinking.

By the term mentor it is acknowledged that it is not just designated teachers who help students to learn. In the Working Lives Project the people interviewed include a toolmaker and a policeman. The teacher reports classroom encounters. The toolmaker's interview includes a question about best moments and he communicates, in speech and manner, something of the joy he finds in producing what 'in the whole history of the universe has never existed before — and I made it!'. The policeman is asked to say something about worst things and, hesitatingly, tells of the loneliness of his wife. 'This', says the teacher, 'draws on knowledge that will not come off the pages of recruitment literature; it is not about "doing tool making" or "being a policeman", but about being a person in the community'. 'I hope and believe', he goes on, 'that there will be some students who will never again be able to dismiss factory workers and the police in stereotypical terms'.

By the term mate, taken from jobmate schemes, a provocative connotation of engendering something new from direct and personal contact on a shared territory is carried. Student reports of the work shadowing at Crofton School convey something of what students gain: 'you become sort of part of it — part of the swing of it'; 'you saw how they live apart from when they are rehearsing — how they often don't get a proper meal, but just have a quick sandwich and chips'; 'I was generally surprised at how musicians regarded it as just another job which they had to do'; 'we saw that they weren't just a disciplined group — we started to see them as a group of individuals and not just as an orchestra'; 'a colossal careers lesson [. . .] it cleared the shadows for me — it let me know what I was really letting myself in for'; 'I thought it was one of the best days of my life, and I would remember it forever'.

By the term politico the fact, reported here, is reflected that it is not just designated leaders who accept responsibility for speaking up for and influencing the future of schooling in our society. Local people's political involvement in the future of Brinnington Community High School (A6) becomes part of the argument for developing its community school status. The loss of political support at Madeley Court School, reported later in this book (B2), proves critical for its ability to maintain community-linked activity.

CAUCUS AND CONSTITUENCY

The frustration of what is held to be a legitimate influence on the action can lead to the formation of yet another role phenomenon of the pre-vocational franchise: membership of a caucus. This is grouping of people taking a joint view on the action. They form with varying degrees of permanence and coherence. Usually, they form in situations of conflict; they often involve speaking, not just for themselves, but as representatives of their audiences in the community: their constituencies.

The Post-Youth Training Scheme Partnerships are formed, in part, explicitly to represent a constituency in the politics of education, a means of counterpoising 'centrist clout' with 'local authority'.

Caucuses and constituencies also appear later in this book. In an account of curriculum development at 'Cloudly' School (B1) a group of teachers develop a joint rationale on the proposal for change which provokes employers on the same planning group to decide that they must now have meetings among themselves off school premises. In the account of Education Work Councils (C1) it is reported that commercial and industrial people hijack some councils as promoters of their interests. In the account of the development of a school-based Community Newspaper Project (D3) department-based teachers consider how they are going to present a consensual case to school management. The work of the 'Elin' School-Community Group (F1), eventually, provokes a commercial and industrial representative to mount an articulate rebuttal of what he takes to be an attack on his constituency. In the development of local liaison groups at County Clare (**F2**) the differences between the style and interests of employment-based, school-based and family-based interests become visible and part of the concern of each.

NEW CLIENTS OF THE FRANCHISE

There are some new gains to be made among the community contacts of the pre-vocational franchise. At a simple level, in City-as-school part of the deal is that community contacts will make use of students as what is acknowledged to be free labour. But there are more penetrating gains to be made, some of which are not envisaged at the outset. In the Transition to Working Life Project it is reported that teachers gain a new sense of the relation between schooling and community and a more adult relation with students. The same project reports that working coaches gain a new respect for young people and discover unexpected resources in themselves. It is also reported that employers notice that working coaches improve their ability to communicate and motivate, in ways which can be used in the workplace, and that trades unionists gain an appreciation of the extent to which unions have lost sight of the experience of young people.

In the Industry Project in Cleveland an employer member of one of the working parties reports that his own relation with his employees has been changed by his participation in community-linked work with a school. In the same project an industrial-relations manager reports, 'I now handle industrial relations differently; I make fewer assumptions about what people mean, I listen more'. A shop steward reports, 'It has made a considerable effect on me; it makes me understand things better; I find myself less hostile to other groups'. Also, in the Cleveland Project, teachers report that working on a teaching pack with trades unionists has helped them to deal with media-induced stereotypes concerning the trades unionist.

Teachers and adults-other-than-teachers can, it seems, become 'learners-other-than-students'.

WHAT KIND OF FRANCHISE?

There is always more than one way of sectioning material to expose it to examination and analysis. But, although different, the resulting analyses are not inconsistent with each other. Figure 1.2 reintegrates them, by showing how different role terms make parallel use of common observations.

Some roles can be contained so that they are relatively uninfluential on the direction of activity: more guests than hosts. Client roles can be like that, so can provisionary roles. Others are harder to contain: they require the sharing of territory and lead to the possibility of initiating departures from established practice. Consultant, developer and mentor can more readily escape the role of guests. A mate is a host on her or his own territory. Some roles have a highly visible influence on the direction of events: politico and manager are examples.

FIGURE 1.2   Linking roles: a comparison of terms

Audience	Promotor	User	Promoter	Audience
– – – – – – – – – – – – –Adults-other-than-teachers – – – – – – – – – – –				
Guest	– – – – – – – – – – – – Host – – – – – – – – – – – – –			Guest
Client				
Provisionary				
Consultant				
Developer				
Mentor				
Mate				
Politico				
Manager				
Constituency member	– – – – – – – –	Caucus member	– – – – – – – –	Constituency member

FOR WHOSE PURPOSES?

The action described in this chapter brings Tom, Dick and Harriet into such influential and, in some cases, visible roles. Caution suggests that selective admissions are made to influential roles. Members of the Chamber of Commerce or the Rotary Club might be felt to be suitable. That will franchise managers of commerce and industry, training and personnel officers and similar 'worthies'.

Usually, the franchise is extended more generously. Parents and past students are recruited as adults-other-than-teachers, the Trades Council is also a source of contact. This enfranchises shop-floor workers from places of employment. There are strong arguments for extending the franchise thus far (see Chapter 6). The Transition to Working Life Project reports that trades unionists make good working coaches.

But some accounts describe the further extension of the franchise. The City-as-school Project is interested in recruiting community-resource people from a wide range of voluntary, media and conservationist activities. The Industry Project in Cleveland actively considers finding adults-other-than-teachers from people interested in the development of alternative forms of work, such as cooperatives, but cannot, finally, agree about this. The Working Lives Project might well open the door to what some people would judge to be the 'grey economy'. An account of the Manningham Centre, given later in the book (C3), makes it a matter of policy to develop partnerships with as full a range as possible of the alternative lifestyles being developed in its inner-city patch.

Enfranchisement may prove to be an irreversible process. Inclusion increases visibility; visibility increases accountability; accountability requires change. In opening the curriculum to community involvement the head of one of the Cleveland schools acknowledges that he is taking a calculated risk. The more potential influence there is in a role the more cautious an organization is likely to be concerning who should be permitted to occupy it. Rewriting social scripts is disturbing.

ACTION
PLANNING LINKS

A part, perhaps the main part, of the problem confronted by the PE teacher described at the beginning of this chapter is that there is no ready-made structure of roles to which he can turn with the threat and opportunity presented by 30 lads standing at the school gates saying 'can we come in?'. He is forced to make on-the-hoof decisions in consultation with whoever he can find who will agree to share responsibility with him concerning what shall be done.

The intention of this chapter, therefore, is to invite you, preferably with colleagues to consider how that supportive structure of roles can be developed to increase the chances of success of any community-linked operation with which you are concerned.

Some of the steps that you might take in such action planning are:

- make a map of the existing boundaries and links in the operation
- state its central concerns
- analyse the roles achieved currently by various of its members
- identify possibilities for role development (new things that could be done or things that could be done by more people)
- where are the major helps and hindrances to those developments?
- in the light of the possibilities, central concern and patterns of help and hindrance, what is the next thing to do?
- who does it?

It will raise at least as many problems as it solves. But this is only the first chapter.

CHAPTER 2

ON LEADING HORSES TO WATER

In this chapter the following are examined critically:

- a method for spotting where, in attempts at educational innovation, there may, and may not, be readiness for change
- an analysis of ideas about what helps and what hinders change
- an examination of some community-linked attempts at innovation and an attempt to spot what went right and what went wrong in the planning and implementation of them
- a method for diagnosis of the next thing to pay attention to in any current attempt to bring about change.

Not all change is a good thing. Is it possible that the great dinosaurs just decided that extinction was preferable to further unacceptable adaptation? They could have had a point! The questions are posed therefore: Where do ideas for acceptable change come from? What is it that makes them acceptable?

It is unlikely that any of the ideas for action described in the last chapter can be imported simply and wholly to any situation known to you. They are not ideal solutions. There are no guaranteed universal solutions.

In the first place, there is no necessary agreement between different groups about the problems to which education is addressed. Secondly, education strategies have a variety of consequences, intended and unintended, anticipated and unanticipated, formal and informal, to which different groups will pay different attention. In the third place, it is sometimes difficult to verify even the intended effects of educational programmes. Fourthly, most educational programmes are highly vulnerable to environmental conditions; some simply won't work in some circumstances. Fifthly, workers in education insist on their right to use any programme selectively, in some part, in some circumstance and in combination with some other programme. Sixthly, they will adapt it; education is a constant process of adjustment, modification and realignment of intention and procedure. In the seventh place, education is an encounter; the nature of the relation between worker and student transforms the impact of the most carefully constructed programme utterly. Lastly, workers may very well have thought out what to do, how to do it and with what materials (and so are just not in the market for programmes imported from elsewhere).

All of this seems to argue for the development of educational programmes at the point of delivery. The workers, better still the students with the workers, should be the researchers, the developers and the evaluators of what is to be provided. It is only in a known place, at a particular time, with an understood group of students that any decision can be made about what should be done.

The rejection of imported development, in favour of locally illuminated suggestions for action, also has its problems. It can be the arbitrary rejection of what is 'not invented here'; that can be merely insular.

In relation to community-linked action the problems of importation will simply not go away, because they entail partnerships which link across boundaries, developing a network in which a variety of perspectives will be represented. People are going to be inviting other people to do things in a different way: there will be disagreements over intentions, other people's ideas will be partially adopted, they will be adapted certainly and different groups will develop their own approaches. Community-linked local innovation does not avoid the problems of importation, it merely relocates them.

The next section invites you to identify whether and how there are helps and hindrances to imported and home-grown innovation in any piece of community-linked innovation with which you have experience.

ACTIVITY

HELPS AND HINDRANCES TO CHANGE

With a colleague, identify attempts at community-linked innovation of which you have first-hand knowledge. Make lists of critical incidents in the progress of events, containing factors which accelerated, advanced, retarded or reversed progress. See if you can agree with a colleague which were which and which factors seem to be most important. To build such accounts with colleagues is useful. Disagreements about what constitute major and minor factors will be underlain by different understandings (theories) concerning what is important in bringing about a change. These understandings will suggest action on any future plan.

If there is sufficient agreement between you it might be possible to cluster the factors into categories. In any event your own list could be headed as follows:

Change factors	
Helping	Hindering
1	1
2	2

The left side gives a list of factors representing readiness for change in a network of contacts. The right-hand list represents unreadiness.

An analysis of factors claimed to be significant in helping and hindering change is given in the following section. These have been clustered into categories: factors in [. . .]

[. . .] the *place* in which innovation occurs
[. . .] the *content* of what is being proposed as a change
[. . .] the *promoters* (persons) who seek to bring the change about
[. . .] the *users* (e.g. teachers) who are expected to go about things in a different way
[. . .] the *clients* (e.g. students) who are expected to get something new from the change
[. . .] *chance* (coincidental) events that make a difference.

The analysis may or may not cause you and a colleague to add to or reorder your own analysis. The point is that you and your colleagues find some way of learning from past experience as a basis for future experience.

INPUT

DIAGNOSIS FOR CHANGE

There is so much that can go wrong in any process of change that it can seem like a miracle that any innovation has ever survived to fruition. The main ways in which things might go wrong are summarized in this section and are distilled from research into educational innovation and, in particular, into school-community linked programmes of change.

Although, at first sight, it seems like a long list of intimidating warnings, it also suggests that there are a number of different sorts of preparation that can be made to give any proposed new action a better chance of survival. It implies that there is no proposal for action which cannot be improved in some respect.

IN THE PLACE

Change does not occur in a vacuum. What is already happening in the place will make a difference to what can happen. The place may be the department, school, college, training programme, working party or network of contacts where the proposal for change is being made.

- How much are people prepared to be influenced by pressure or argument from outside the group? How satisfied are they with their own view of the situation? Open *boundary maintenance* is generally more ready for change than closed boundary maintenance.
- Is what is done in one part of the outfit known, understood and appreciated by other parts? Are people cut off from questioning and support from partners? Extensive *cross-communication* generally supports more change than does limited cross-communication.

- Do people know who make the decisions; can they influence and participate in that process? Or is decision-making a separated prerogative of a few? Accessible *decision making* generally brings about more change than inaccessible decision making.
- Is time, money, materials and equipment allocated, volunteered or negotiated to support the change? Or will it increase pressure on resources? Finding slack in *resourcing* is more supportive of change than allowing change to increase the pressure.

IN THE ACTION

Some suggestions for change will prove more acceptable to any outfit than others. The content and presentation of suggested action will have features which give it greater or lesser chances of being taken up.

- Is what is being suggested something which corresponds with preoccupations and intentions among the people to be involved? Is it something out of the blue and unrelated to what concerns them? Action that identifies a high degree of *common ground* with current concerns is more likely to survive than action which makes low a degree of common ground.
- Have people been given a chance to understand what is being proposed: rationale and operation? Is there confusion? Presentations which give people every chance to achieve *clarity* stand a better chance of acceptance.

IN THE PROMOTER

Few changes occur unless some person or persons do something to make them happen. The way in which such promoters go about influencing others will make a difference to whether and how the proposed action will be taken up.

- There is more than one way to influence other people: demanding, bargaining, inspiring, supporting and informing action call on different styles. How varied are the styles used by promoters? How rigidly do they stick to one style? Varied *styles* are usually more influential than a rigid style.
- Is what is said to promote the action tailored (negotiated) to meet the needs and interests of different groups of people whose support is sought? Is everybody treated as though their needs and interests are the same as everybody else's? Negotiated *communication* is usually more effective than unnegotiated.
- How much opportunity are people given to meet and talk with promoters, so that they can, in personal terms, see, hear, recognize and respond to what is being promoted? Is the promotion impersonal? Personal *social skills* are usually more effective than impersonal promotions of change.
- Influence can be bold (radical, pushy, in-a-hurry) or it can be cautious (careful, laid-back, one-thing-at-a-time); is influence flexible, judged according to what is possible and needed? Do promoters adopt either pushy or laid-back postures habitually? Flexible *influence management* has more to offer to the possibilities for change than habitual influence management.

IN THE USERS

Change means that people are going to do something new or do something differently. These users of the change will make a difference to whether and how it is implemented.

- Have the users taken on board the 'why?', 'what?' and 'how?' of what is being proposed? Or not? A surprising number of innovations fail because users do not gain a sufficient *understanding* of what they are being asked to do.
- Can they do it, in terms of the time, materials, experience and skill available to them? Or is there no match between the proposal and the resources available to users? Matched *resources* give innovation a better chance of survival.
- How do they feel about it?: enthusiastic? committed? convinced of its relevance? ready and willing? or not? Guess what happens to innovations where user *attitudes* are negative.
- In how many senses can the proposal be said to be the 'property' of the users: do they suggest it, or any part of it, or comment on it, or revise it? Or are they being asked to carry other people's baggage? Where *participation* is low, it is 'not theirs', and the consequences for implementation are negative.

IN THE CLIENTS

Somebody is expected to gain something from the change; these may be called its clients. They are usually, but not necessarily, students. They may be teachers, parents, employers or anyone in the network of contacts. Clients make a difference to the impact of change.

- Do clients have a grasp of what is being offered, of why, and of how they can get the best from it? Or is it just something else to be done? Where client *preparedness* is high, both in terms of an overview of the action and each of its specific parts, then innovation has a better chance both of survival and effectiveness.
- Can clients relate it to their needs? Or is it just something else that has to be accepted? Aside from the fact that we don't have resources to waste on irrelevant proposals, a proposal to which clients can feel no *relatedness* is more likely to be resisted than one perceived as relevant.
- On the assumption that clients know what they can get from the action, do they have a chance to reflect on whether and how those gains have been made? Or, when any part of the action is completed, do we all rush on to the next thing to do? *Reflectiveness*, a chance to reflect on how it has paid off (in terms of learning and other benefits), is likely to be more penetrating in its effect and be more acknowledged as worthwhile.

BY CHANCE

Sometimes it is what nobody could have anticipated that proves to be a critical factor in the progress of change.

- What unforeseen event has obstructed movement? What has offered an opportunity? Some *critical incidents* offer obstruction and opportunity simultaneously.

EXAMPLES

WHAT CAN BE DONE?

Two examples of attempts to implement community-linked changes in schools are given in the following pages. They are analysed to identify all the factors for change mentioned previously. They can be used fruitfully by working with colleagues on suggestions about where the most effective action might be taken to maximize the chances that something worthwhile will be sustained.

Indications of the significance that can be attached to each part of the analyses have been entered on five-point scales:

(1) *danger*, there is something to hinder the programme here
(2) *careful*, there could be something to hinder the programme here
(3) *hopeful*, maybe there's nothing to be concerned about, but more could have been done
(4) *promising*, looks good
(5) *ready*, it's hard to see what more can be done to advance matters.

There are other examples charted in Table 2.1, all of which refer to some factors for change.

B1   Curriculum Development in 'Cloudly' School

The intention is to introduce a research and development-based piece of careers education curriculum into the school. The programme is a response to student views on existing career educational programmes in the school and elsewhere. Those responses suggest the design of a programme which is intellectually demanding, developing coherently from experience to experience and engaging students in direct and personal contact with adult and working life in the community. The pack is designed to be used over a 6-week period of two careers lessons a week, with fifth formers. It is designed to lead students into active use of an ensuing work-experience placement. It comprises a rationale, an explanation of method, and classroom materials.

The main promoter of the idea outside the school is a project officer from the college where the programme has been developed. He works in close cooperation with the pastoral deputy who is highly committed to getting the programme implemented.

The place

Boundary maintenance

A commerce- and industry-linked working party is established at the suggestion of the project team to monitor progress and make suggestions. The project worker reports difficulty in meeting school staff. After vigorous arguments are mounted against the programme, the industrial and commercial representatives on the working party elect to meet outside school.

careful

---

closed   open

Cross-communication
Split sites do not help. A late substitute chairperson to the first working party meeting is reported to know little about the proposed programme.

	careful	
limited		extensive

Decision making
The head delegates contact with the programme to the pastoral deputy, and — because of the pastoral deputy's illness — to the curriculum deputy.

	hopeful	
inaccessible		accessible

Resourcing
Time for careers education work is being cut. It is hoped that fifth-year periods will survive the cuts.

	careful	
tight		slack

The action

Common ground
The programme has been designed by a project team based in a college. Its rationale is the evidence from research of student feedback, and an argument for the necessity in careers education for students to be helped each to find, sift and analyse each his or her own way of looking at work.

	danger	
low		high

Clarity
A rationale and description is written out, circulated and discussed. There is no suggestion that people are not clear about what is being proposed.

	promising	
vague		clear

The promoters

Style
Heavy reliance is place on the rationale for the programme. When he is confronted with opposition, the research officer elaborates the rationale for the programme.

	careful	
rigid		varied

Communication
The project officer meets the head, the pastoral deputy, the careers teacher and all the industrial and commercial representatives, talking them through the existing written rationale for the programme.

	careful	
unnegotiated		negotiated

Social skill
The project officer visits the school frequently. In particular he offers to demonstrate the running of the programme so that the doubtful careers teacher can assess his own approach to it.

	promising	
impersonal		personal

Influence management
As an occasional visitor the project officer is in no position to give the programme a strong push. The pastoral deputy is hampered by illness. Faced with sustained opposition the pastoral deputy does not confront it. He reports that his previous attempts at curriculum development have not yet been successful.

	careful	
habitual		flexible

The users

Understanding
The rationale has been discussed with the teacher expected to use it. There is no suggestion that opposition or misuse is a consequence of misunderstanding.

	promising	
no		yes

Resources
The programme is designed to draw on conventional classroom management skills. There is a written description of procedures, which have been talked through with the teacher expected to use them. The teacher expresses concern about not having enough time to prepare.

	hopeful	
unmatched		matched

Attitude
Teachers are reported to show less enthusiasm for the programme than commercial and industrial representatives on the working party. Some teachers say that the programme is too orientated to employment in this area of high unemployment. The curriculum deputy characterizes the programme as 'middle class', failing to take account of what students already know, likely to be a subtle form of indoctrination and to raise their hopes falsely.

	danger	
negative		positive

Participation
The programme is in all its essentials ready-made by the time the teachers who are to use it see it.

	danger	
not theirs		theirs

The clients

Preparedness

The programme is designed to equip students for forth-coming work-experience programme. The method is interactive, inviting student participation. No preparatory work is, however, reported which gives students an overall view of the programme.

	careful	
unprepared		prepared

Relatedness

The programme is based on feedback covering the career relevance of schooling gained from students — some of whom are in this school. But given a choice between this programme and extra English, about 50 per cent of clientele opt for English.

	careful	
irrelevant		relevant

Reflectiveness

Each stage of the programme invites students to reflect on their own and each other's understandings of work. Each student makes and keeps a record of her or his developing picture of working life.

		promising
no chance		every chance

Chance

Critical incident

The pastoral deputy is ill on the day of the first working party meeting. The curriculum deputy takes over at short notice.

	careful	
obstruction		opportunity

The programme is run by the project officer, not — as intended — the careers teacher. The working party does not continue to meet in school and only occasionally in premises outside. Some of the experience-based contacts identified for use by the programme are used by one of the teachers for other purposes. Objections to the programme are sustained; for example by one teacher who worries about placing certain students 'near money'. Perceived lack of cooperation eventually persuades the pastoral deputy to curtail the programme.

Source: Roberts and Law, 1985.

B2   Madeley Court School

The intention is to integrate the existing school with the education and recreation centre with which it shares a site.

The school is already organized as 'mini-schools' in years 1–3. Each mini-school is a self-managed unit, with its own staff, area, timetable and resources, and with sustained cross-curricular contact with its students for half their time at school. Timetabling in the senior school is designed to encourage interdepartmental cooperation. The current proposal is a response to perceptions of piecemeal provision for members of the community; information, help, facilities and support coming from different agencies acting more-or-less independently of each other. The concern is sharpened by perceptions of special need in this area of high unemployment. It is focused by the fact that unemployed past students return to the school to hang about because they have nothing to do. The proposal is for integrated provision of leisure, education, support, accommodation and consultative facilities on a single site, to be supplemented with help drawn from local professional and voluntary services. There is also to be a shop, a bar, a restaurant, a camp site, etc.

It is the head, in close consultation with kindred thinkers on the senior staff, who is most actively promoting the idea. LEA rejection of the proposal leads to the compromise implementation of a school-based community curriculum.

The place

Boundary maintenance
The school is timetabled to permit sustained periods of community contact. A community-linked working party is established to develop the proposal.

	ready
closed	open

Cross-communication
The school is organized on cross-curricular lines, especially in years 1–3. Weekly consultations are held between heads of departments and mini-school staff. There are twice-a-term early closures to provide for half-day 'in-service discussion'.

	ready
limited	extensive

Decision making
Week-to-week decision making is vested in mini-school and cross-curricular teams; strategic decision making is in public forum. Decisions take account of staff concerns, on this basis mini-school organization is not extended to years 4 and 5.

	ready
inaccessible	accessible

Resourcing
Pilot development uses temporary government-funded workers. A commitment of 5 years funding is negotiated with the development corporation, but continuation will require LEA commitment.

	hopeful
tight	slack

The action

Common ground
The proposal is contrary to LEA policy for the school. Politicians are either hostile or passive. Much — but not all — of the staff is supportive. Some opposition is addressed in a letter to the governors.

	danger
low	high

Clarity
There is no suggestion that people do not understand
what is being proposed.

hopeful

vague   clear

The promoters

Style
Progress is sought by means of argument, evidence and
consultation in working parties, discussion groups and
staff development activity.

promising

rigid   varied

Communication
Arguments are mounted in a way which responds to the
concerns of staff; but there is no evidence of canvassing
the idea outside the staff, parents and governors of the
school — for example, among politicians and officers of
the LEA.

careful

unnegotiated   negotiated

Social skill
The head is perceived as authentic — is liked and admired
by those with whom he works most closely.

promising

impersonal   personal

Influence management
The head is an idealogue: there are certain issues on which
he will not compromise. He is also persistent and bold.
The cross-curricular reorganization of the school is a bold
move.

careful

habitual   flexible

The users

Understanding
Teachers voluntarily become involved in the programme
— developing its ideology in pilot and compromise forms.

promising

no   yes

Resources
The head acknowledges that too-radical innovation may
de-skill some teachers, but many get involved. Time is
made for staff-development activity.

promising

unmatched   matched

Attitude
Staff commitment is judged by HMI to be high, but some
staff have resigned.

hopeful

negative   positive

Participation
The details of specific provisions within the programme
are worked out by teachers.

	promising	
not theirs		theirs

The clients

Preparedness
There are learning objectives for different aspects of the
compromise programme. Students participate in conferences making school and community resources visible.
Students help prepare a bulletin updating facilities
available.

	promising	
unprepared		prepared

Relatedness
The plan is, in part, a response to perceived needs. Pilot
development establishes useability and engenders hope for
expansion. Parents, students and governors are welcom-
ing to the idea.

	promising	
irrelevant		relevant

Reflectiveness
Plans that are put into school-based operation are linked
to learning objectives, the achievement of which is recorded by students.

	promising	
no chance		every chance

Chance

Critical incident
Government-funding provides staff for pilot implementation, but more will be needed for full-scale
implementation.

	hopeful	
obstruction		opportunity

Critical incident
At a critical stage of showdown new governors are
appointed, leaving the head without an important source
of 'constituency' support.

danger		
obstruction		opportunity

During the 'compromise' phase the idea of community curriculum opens up the school theatre to
the neighbourhood, sixth-form accommodation to become a youth club, the home-economics area
as an 'under 5s' unit and the staff room to local senior citizens who want to drop in. An adult-
education programme is launched. The school establishes a range of income-earning student-run
enterprises, school premises host conventions, conferences and fairs in which students, staff and
local people share. Persistent LEA concerns with 'standards' in the school finally lead to an HMI
report. It finds good attendance, good student–teacher relations, a wide range of extra curricular

activities, strong staff commitment. But it also finds 'low standards'. The head is called before the governors and told that his 'interests and concerns with the relation between the school and local social and recreational provision' must wait while the concerns of HMI are dealt with. The head feels that to continue will involve unacceptably compromising his professional ideology. He resigns.

Sources: Watts, 1983; Toogood, 1984; Fletcher *et al.*, 1985.

Table 2.1 charts an analysis of all examples of community-linked activity described in this chapter and elsewhere in this book. They are analysed according to whether the descriptions of action touch on issues for the six factors for change just referred to: *place, content, promoters, users, clients* and *chance*.

The table also analyses the material according to where the ideas for action originate. The analysis is related to the distinction made previously between home grown and imported development. But that distinction clearly is too simple. The analysis is therefore fourfold. The entries are classified: *user*, where responsibility is accepted wholly by the people implementing the action; *institution*, where that responsibility is an institutional one, with management making the idea an accountable part of the organization's work; *consultancy*, where users and institution seek help from people based outside the institution in the development of ideas; *community*, where they are developed outside the institution by a community-based group which seeks to influence what happens in school, college or programme; *imported*, where the ideas are taken substantially from sources remote from the point of delivery.

Accounts can be found in other chapters as follows: A in Chapter 1; C in Chapter 3; D in Chapter 4; F in Chapter 7.

TABLE 2.1 Changing schooling : examples of different originations and reported factors for help and hindrance

Reported factors	Origination				
	User	Institution	Consultancy	Community	Imported
Place	A7, D3	A6, B2, C2, C3	A3, D1, F3	D1, F2	B1
Content	A7, D3	A2, A6, B2, C2, D2, C3	A3, A4, D1, F3	A5, C1, D1, F1, F2	B1
Promoters	A7, D3	A2, A6, B2, C2, D2, C3	A3, A4, D1, F3	A5, C1, D1, F1, F2	B1
Users	A7, D3	A2, A6, B2, C2, C3	A3, A4, D1, F3	C1, D1, F1, F2	B1
Clients	A1, A7, D3	A6, B2, C2, C3	A3, A4, F3	F2	B1
Chance	D3	B2	D1		B1

EXPLORATION

SECOND THOUGHTS ON CHANGE

WHOSE RESPONSIBILITY?

Innovation in schooling, in all its stages, has come under intensifying scrutiny. An ultimate concern will be with what students can gain: a concern with the effectiveness. However, a current criticism of research into the conditions for effective schooling (e.g. Rutter *et al.*, 1979) is that they pay little attention to 'how the factors operate or how to implement them in a particular school' and that 'they say nothing about the dynamics of the organization' (Fullan, 1985); that is the more immediate concern here: with how innovation gains acceptance in schooling, a concern with survivability. It entails asking about how new curriculum is developed and achieves impact, how the attitudes and behaviour of users develop, how consultancy and organization-development techniques contribute and what happens in useful processes of evaluation and accountability.

Not surprisingly, there is no dominant diagnosis for success or failure. Change comes from a series of interdependent events, in which developers, users, clients, managers and audiences share. This is how change within any organic community is now seen, the ecological unfolding, over time, of a multiplicity of dependencies between inhabitants. This understanding has the effect of making talk of the 'if only [. . .]' type appear simple minded ('if only the head would [. . .]', 'if only there was more money for [. . .]', 'if only training could be given to [. . .]').

There is no dominant diagnosis, but there are recurring observations. The analysis given previously in this chapter collates those observations into a single series of headings (an earlier version of which appears in Roberts and Law, 1985). One of the features of the analysis is that it exempts nobody from responsibility.

CHANGE IN ITS PLACE

Most studies pay attention to the context in which the change is to occur. The context is the organizational and social ambience and structure into which change is introduced and the beliefs, attitudes and behaviours which prevail there. Features of context identified here are boundary maintenance, cross-communication, decision making and resourcing.

BOUNDARY MAINTENANCE

Boundary maintenance refers to how the organization does and does not link to what happens outside. It is a concept with obvious relevance to pre-vocational education. Open boundary maintenance means visibility, cooperation, travel and influence between inside and outside. Studies concerned with hindrances to change have identified the invisibility of teachers in their roles inside the school and the relative weakness of attempts by people outside the boundary to influence what happens inside (Havelock, 1973). The opening of boundaries is reported to be resisted because it requires inside professionals to share their responsibility and influence and because it risks disturbing stable consensus (Evans and Law, 1984). Studies concerned with what helps have developed notions such as 'responsive accountability', in which occurs 'free and open communication with a variety of interest groups about the aims of and nature of education' (Elliott, 1981). This notion explicitly rejects negotiation with a single caucus outside the organization, which could mean merely the support of an unaccountable inside power with another outside one.

CROSS-COMMUNICATION

Cross-communication refers to the extent to which members of an organization are in touch with each other. Reported hindrances include the separation of colleagues from each other (Havelock, 1973) and lack of opportunity for sharing information, building cooperation, ameliorating fears and changing attitudes (Morrish, 1976). Reported helping factors are where members share support, trust, acceptance and confidence (Watson, 1967), team-building activity (Fullan and Pomfret, 1977), collective problem solving (Fullan et al., 1981), opportunities for mutual observation and the chance to talk about the process of teaching (Fullan, 1985).

DECISION MAKING

Decision making refers to how the choices confronting the organization are handled. Some regard the support of the hierarchy as an important, even necessary, condition for change (Watson, 1967; Fullan and Pomfret, 1977). This is because the hierarchy can release resources (Evans and Law, 1984) and because workers will not feel mandated, or even encouraged, unless they can see that their participation is supported by management (Davies, 1981). The support of management is argued to be important, not only to get things started, but at all subsequent stages (Fullan et al., 1981). Yet management involvement can be hindering: where suggestions for change from 'above' can be interpreted as reflections on the adequacy and efficiency of users, leaving them with options of defensiveness, powerlessness or perversity (Havelock, 1973). There are accounts of management-mandated change failing because, with 'political naivety', it tries to bypass consultation with users, concerning the acceptability and feasibility of the innovation (Fullan and Pomfret, 1977). The support of management guarantees nothing. A more subtle characterization of decision making begins to emerge, voiced as 'a feel for the process', acknowledging its complexity and not expecting to be able to preplan step-by-step decision making; it portrays the organization as 'sailed not driven' (Fullan, 1985), balancing, so to speak, the 'rudder' of management against the 'wind and currents' of user's influence.

RESOURCING

Resourcing refers to the organization's provision of time, materials, money, space and personnel to the operation. Among reported hindrances to change are overburdened personnel, too preoccupied with present concerns to consider new ones (Havelock, 1973). Among reported requirements is 'resource slack' (Fullan, 1972); which continues to be available beyond pump priming, because there are frequently residual and unanticipated needs. It is not just a matter of gaining new resources but of handling existing resources flexibly, so that 'the organization should be adaptive with enough flexibility to change timetables, groupings and so on, as necessary (McMahon *et al.*, 1984). Progress has been reported to be enhanced where at least part of the resourcing originates inside the organization, rather than relying wholly on external help (Fullan *et al.*, 1981). Part of the argument for sustained resourcing is because users need an opportunity to reflect on their first-phase involvement; this period of reflection identifies further resource requirements (Fullan and Pomfret, 1977). Some reports suggest that a minimal expenditure of resources on a development might actually do more harm than good, uncovering problems and setting up expectations, but actually unable to resolve or deliver anything (Fullan *et al.*, 1981).

AGREEING THE ACTION

A good many studies include accounts of how proposals for 'this' rather than 'that' action come to be implemented. The two considerations identified here are, first, the extent of common ground made between the proposal and concerns in the organization and, secondly, the clarity with which the proposal is put forward.

COMMON GROUND

Common ground refers to the overlap that exists between what members of the organization can identify as worthwhile action and what is actually proposed. Common ground is high where members of the organization can recognize value in what is being proposed; it is low if they perceive it as pointless. It raises questions about who has what control over the origination of ideas for action. One distinction is between what are called research, development and diffusion (RDD) and problem-solving (PS) models for change. Extreme forms of RDD put the origination of the project beyond the influence of users and audiences in the organization. Needs are researched, solutions are found or developed and dissemination occurs, independently of the organization in which use is to occur, whereas in pure PS members of the organization are asked to identify needs and suggest and develop responses for themselves. Outside help restricts itself to putting knowledge, material and consultancy at the disposal of a process which is controlled by people in the place of implementation. The resulting proposal for action will therefore originate inside the organization; it will reflect host values, it will be 'owned' there and its people will understand it. The views of audiences as well as users are important because any proposal for action, even action in somebody else's department, will change the ethos in which all participants work (Fullan, 1985).

Commonly, it is reported that PS is more likely to produce effective and durable change (Miles, 1967; Watson, 1967; Morrish, 1976) and that this is because any outside consultant will 'avoid transmitting messages [. . .] which devalue established practice and [. . .] self-esteem' (MacDonald and Walker, 1976). Suggested change will then 'be centrally relevant to the members of the target user group and bring major benefits to them; and [. . .] have underlying values that are congruent with those of the target group, particularly the teachers, pupils and their parents' (McMahon *et al.*, 1984). At first sight PS might seem like a recipe for action which would have gone down well in the Third

Reich, but proponents do not intend that perspectives from beyond the organization's 'Oder' and 'Rhine' will be excluded. It is a matter of both 'reassuring practitioners' and yet not 'buttressing previous practice' (MacDonald and Walker, 1976). In any event, it is reported also that change initiated externally can work well and may, indeed, be essential if anything is to happen at all (Fullan, 1985). What unifies these observations is not the support they give to origination inside the organization unconditionally, but to changes suggested, whatever their origins may be, which overlap significantly with the concerns of users and audiences in the host organization.

CLARITY

Clarity refers to the extent to which what is being proposed is presented in a way which enables people to understand what it is, what it is for and how it works. Lack of clarity in planning has been known to affect outcomes adversely (Stenhouse, 1975; Morrish, 1976); a failure to identify and differentiate concerns and intentions is reported to hinder the progress of innovation (Evans and Law, 1984). It is reported that a common reason for failure is that the people who are expected to do the work have been given too little opportunity to understand its rationale or procedure (Fullan, 1972). Among the helpful strategies identified is an opportunity for users to make the innovation explicit to themselves (Fullan and Pomfret, 1977). What is proposed should 'be simple and flexible, so that teachers can understand what they have to do, so that the innovation can be broken down into components parts, and — most important — so that the innovation can be adapted to the needs of local circumstances' (McMahon *et al.*, 1984).

PROMOTING CHANGE

Studies also describe a variety of means whereby people who get things changed go about that work. This promoter's style, communication skill, social skill and influence management all seem to be worth attending to.

STYLE

Style refers to the repertoire for influence on which promoters draw. Positional influence is available to people who can set up a legitimate expectation that 'this is what is going to happen'. Exchange influence negotiates on a 'if you will [. . .] I will [. . .]' basis. Personal influence brings about movement on the basis of attachment to the person who suggests it. Consultative influence reflects with people on problems they, as clients, identify, until a solution emerges. Expert influence argues a rational case, based on evidence. Different styles have different effects on different settings; different users find different styles congenial to their way of learning (Handy, 1976). The styles used should be multiple, identified in one report as being 'perceived favourably by the target user group' (personal influence?), as having 'the right "status"' (positional influence?), as having 'authority' (expert influence?), as having 'leadership style', as well as, ideally, a 'successful "track record"' in the implementation of innovations' (McMahon *et al.*, 1984). Tall order! It raises a question about whether the promotion of any complex or radical action can ever be handled by one promoter. It argues difficulty for promoters who, rigidly, sing only one song in the repertoire of influence.

COMMUNICATION SKILL

Communication skill refers to the way in which promoters select the content and form of what they say; it identifies issues for what to say, and what not to say, in presenting a case to others. It has been observed that successful change has been brought about by promoters of an RDD project, who solve their communication problems, not by saying everything more clearly or more often, but by altering the content of communication so that it sounds more like what specific audiences want to hear. They do not lie, nor are they consistent with themselves; they are just careful about what they say to whom (MacDonald and Walker, 1976). This could be RDD with a winning smile and a careful tongue!

SOCIAL SKILL

Social skill refers to presentation of ideas for action personally. A strategy for change that is sometimes interposed as a median position between RDD and PS, is social interaction (SI). In it a promoter brings new ideas for action, which may not ever have occurred to the users, presented through personal contact. All the stages of gaining an understanding of what is being proposed (reacting to it, identifying difficulties, working out solutions) are therefore negotiated personally and within some control by the user. It entails the setting up of networks of personal contact (MacDonald and Walker, 1976). In some cases the skills required by the project are modelled by the promoters, so that potential users can see what is being asked of them (MacDonald and Walker, 1976). A parallel finding emerges from a report on what teachers learn from in-service training, part of which is the observation of trainers doing what they are talking about (Law, 1977b). It is suggested that a useful strategy for bringing about change in organizations and, as far as schools are concerned, one that is largely lacking, is a 'change agent' who can introduce and demonstrate new ideas in personal contact with the users (Havelock, 1973). It is becoming a common feature of change strategies that an internal coordinator is appointed, part of whose role it is to represent the existence and resources of the project to users and audiences in the schools (Davies, 1981). Some argue that, even where outside consultants are brought in, an inside contact, who can maintain day-to-day contact with staff, is a considerable advantage (Fullan *et al.*, 1981).

INFLUENCE MANAGEMENT

Influence management refers to the way in which the promoter balances her or his influence with others'. Some reports characterize the achievement of this balance as 'political skill and an orientation to working with power relationships' (Fullan *et al.*, 1981). Teachers, in reporting on relations with outside advisers, emphasize the importance of tact and discretion; they 'wished to be responsible for their own actions and were not happy to think an outsider was taking decisions for them: yet some want advisers to offer "harder", "more searching", "deeper", "more critical" comments — to have "a bit more bite"' (Elliott *et al.*, 1981). Bite and tact are not automatically reconcilable postures. One sustained account of the work of an outside adviser poses a dilemma concerning whether he should go ahead on the basis of initially identified concerns or go back to the organization to provoke more discussion of what he suspects is not-very-astringently finished business. His initial reaction is 'the passive one', but, he claims, he becomes 'a more interventionist "chaser"' as his doubts about the basis for action persist (Davies, 1981). A study of guidance specialists identifies a role as change agent in schools and indicates that they speak of the resolution of its dilemmas with a preference for, or an avoidance of, interventionist action (Law, 1979). The use of pressure in the promotion of change is acknowledged, but pressure which is exercised 'in interaction with the users' (Fullan, 1985). Project reports identify the need for continuously reviewed judgement on relating one's own authority to the authority of other people; speaking of a concern with scaling, interventions to the condition of the client (Evans and Law, 1984) or deciding when to come forward with an idea or suggestion and when to pull back and give clients room to work out their own positions and reactions (Roberts and Law, 1985). Most of these reports suggest a need to balance influence somewhere between boldness (referred to as bite, chasing, intervention, pressure, coming forward) and caution (referred to as tact, discretion, interaction with clients, pulling back and leaving room for clients). Many of them suggest that knowing how to achieve that balance depends on an understanding of the readiness of the users and audiences for what is being proposed.

USE OF THE ACTION

In most accounts of change attention is paid to the experience of people who are expected to do something different, or differently, to implement the change. Observations can be sorted for their reference to users' understanding, resources, attitudes and participation.

UNDERSTANDING

Understanding refers to the extent to which the users have a clear idea of what the innovation means. A recurring problem for innovation is reported to be users who are unable to say in any clear way what the essential principles of the innovation are; they are doing it with little understanding of why they are doing it. New action, it is argued, is implemented too frequently on the basis of old understanding: habitual thinking which is reinforced day-to-day in schools and which it is difficult to dismantle and re-examine (Fullan, 1972). An analysis of later data leads to the observation that 'the most fundamental breakthrough occurs when people can cognitively understand the underlying conceptions and rationale with respect to "why this new way works better"' (Fullan, 1985).

RESOURCES

Resources refer to the capacity of the users to deliver the action. Capacity means enough time and material, and the appropriate position and skills. Needed resources are reported to be commonly underestimated by management (Fullan, 1985). Suggestions for new action need to be within the capacities of users (Morrish, 1976) and 'feasible in terms of its costs and its implications for teachers — for example, concerning their status and job definition, and in not requiring too much extra work and time' (McMahon *et al.*, 1984). Lack of skill is reported to be a problem for some implementation (Fullan and Pomfret, 1977). Awkwardness with new operations and the sheer novelty of the operation have been reported as blocks to acceptance (Fullan, 1985; Roberts and Law, 1985). A significant skill of outside consultants is that of matching suggestions to skills in which users already have some confidence (Roberts and Law, 1985). The skills of users are, however, potential as well as actual; where intensive in-service training, as distinct from single workshops or pre-service training, is provided, programmes are reported to be more likely to succeed (Fullan and Pomfret, 1977). Training should include an examination of theory, the demonstration of operations and, importantly, practice, feedback and coaching in operations; it should also be designed to increase mastery of the innovation over a period of time progressively (Fullan, 1985). But training, however effective it may be, does little to improve the availability of the users' time, the provision of materials or the appropriateness of their position.

ATTITUDES

Attitudes refers to the disposition which users have to the proposed change. It is reported that users need to retain a strong sense of both autonomy and security in working with a new programme; attempts to impose ready-made programmes for adoption by users can threaten those needs (Watson, 1967). Yet users, it is argued, should be 'receptive to change, have high staff morale [. . .] and ready to expend extra effort' (McMahon *et al.*, 1984). Attitudes can be changed by in-service training, but such changes do not seem to survive the heat of re-entry to institutionalized schooling indefinitely (Law, 1979). It is the early months of a new programme which are reported to be fraught particularly with anxiety and confusion, but these are reported to subside as mastery of the rationale and procedures are found; in other words 'changes in attitudes, beliefs and understandings tend to follow rather than precede changes in behaviour' (Fullan, 1985).

PARTICIPATION

Participation refers to the level of involvement that users have in the shaping of the programme. Among the reported explanations of innovative failure is the urging of generalized methods and procedures on users, with a failure to take account of the needs specifically to adapt any existing programme and to create new programmes to fit specific situational needs (Havelock, 1973). Organization development programmes are reported to be more effective where staff share in the decision making about whether or not to go ahead with them (Fullan *et al.*, 1981). Curriculum developments are more likely to be implemented successfully where teachers are involved in initiating, adapting, planning and operationalizing the innovation (Fullan and Pomfret, 1977). The help that users give each other, in that process, proves to be as significant a source of help as that provided by outside consultants (Fullan, 1985). Suggestions should therefore 'provide opportunities for members of the target user group to develop and modify the innovation locally; by adapting materials, by learning what the innovation will involve and to develop a sense of 'owning it' (McMahon *et al.*, 1984). But there are some kinds of innovation where such participation may not be useful; that is where the innovation is fully developed and requires faithful adoption of all its design features. In such cases a decisive managerial strategy may be required (Fullan and Pomfret, 1977; Fullan, 1985).

GAINING FROM CHANGE

Few studies of the survivability of change refer to the impact on change of students. Yet much of what is written about proposals for change relates it explicitly to the needs of students, as though we have first studied our clients and are relating what we propose to our understanding of them. In some, not all, cases such argumentation invites scepticism; where, for example, the needs of students resembles suspiciously a transposed list of provisions of teachers: a bad case of projection posturing as empathy (see Fawcett, 1985). Teachers, however, cannot escape exposure to the reactions of students; a plausible theory of curriculum development can include acknowledgement of the fact that we tend to change what we do with students when we find that they won't sit still for what we were doing before. This section is based on the assumption that the gains that students are able to make from innovation will make a difference to its survivability. The assumption requires only an acknowledgement that students can shape teacher behaviour; their participation in terms of preparedness, relatedness and reflectiveness is analysed.

PREPAREDNESS

Preparedness refers to the extent to which clients know what is being offered, what to expect, how they can get ready for it and what they can gain from it. It means the clarification and declaration of objectives with students so that they know whether, when and how they are achieving them. Where students are invited to pursue foreseeable gains, rather than merely to engage in 'something to be got done and out of the way', then, it seems plausible to suggest, impact will be strengthened. The modularization of courses into units of work is, in part, to help students foresee and pursue achievable objectives purposefully.

RELATEDNESS

Relatedness refers to the extent to which clients can relate what they can gain to what they need. It means developing, by enquiry, alertness and reflection, an understanding of the here-and-now and foreseeable life experience of students; this is a matter on which the perceptions of teachers and the perceptions of students have, sometimes, been reported to be at variance (Bazalgette, 1978). Surveys of change that draw on commercial and industrial analogies celebrate the adaptability of firms which are 'close to the customer' (Fullan, 1985). Also studies of the effectiveness of schooling have identified sharing experience with students, and giving students a say in their schooling, as features of effective schools (Rutter *et al.*, 1979). Such reports suggest the importance to any innovative programme of teacher and student working together to identify the match and mismatch between what they do in schooling and what they need in experience. It is not argued here that instant recognizability by students should be the sole criterion for change in schooling, but, where they can see a relation between their experience and gains to be made, then the survivability of the programme will be strengthened, at least in the sense that they are more likely to show up for it.

REFLECTIVENESS

Reflectiveness refers to the extent to which clients can re-examine what they have learned; disclosing, reviewing, articulating, comparing, collating, conceptualizing, and examining critically their gains from schooling. It rebalances the relative importance given by teachers to the tasks of 'telling' and the tasks of asking 'how are you getting on with that'. All the existing apparatus of student-centred reviewing, and the processing of disclosure after experiential and experience-based schooling, is an elaboration of that task.

CHANCE

The fact that unintended and unforeseen events impact the progress of innovation is not mentioned much in studies of change. But people become ill, leave and new people connect with the action, with unforeseeable consequences. Where they are documented it is pointed out that a chance event can be both 'lucky' and 'unlucky' (Roberts and Law, 1985). The 'unfreezing' of the situation which chance events provoke can provide quick-thinking developers with the material for an on-the-hoof opportunity which, in some reported cases, has proved decisive. Operations that rely on the participation of inside and outside contacts, not all of whom have formal membership of the institution, may prove to be exposed particularly to chance events. Indeed a report of one such networking operation, where community contacts are in a continuous and unpredictable process of being made and broken, characterized it as 'management by opportunity', making the availability of changing resources a mainspring of decision making in the organization (Law, 1982).

CONCLUSIONS

No proposal for new action in schooling has had, as far as anybody has been able to verify, everything going for it. When the sheer ecological complexity of the process is examined it seems close-to-miraculous that any have survived, let alone been effective. Where plots on scales like those suggested in the examples section of this chapter fall to the left consistently, proposition of change might seem like a route to a coronary or paranoia, or both.

But that is only a possible implication, not a certain one. More certain is the fact that no two organizations will implement any innovation in the same way. There are too many variables. The implication of that is that, although nothing is ever perfectly ready, neither is anything perfectly unready for change. Indeed, there does appear to be a 'critical mass' of readiness for change: a minimum requirement, if movement is to occur. That critical mass will in all but a minority of cases be attainable.

The task, then, is to diagnose the specific situation in such a way as to identify where the greatest increase in that critical mass can best be achieved. That means the use of such an analysis to spot where best next action is indicated. It is a judgement that will vary with where the greatest hindrances are located, where the best hope of movement is indicated and who is to undertake the action. For the analysis has two features worth highlighting: there is never only one thing that can be done to improve the chances of suggested innovation and there is never only one person who can undertake that action.

ACTION
WHERE TO START?

The critical-mass theory of innovation in education contains three propositions: (1) nothing is perfect (people who wait for perfect conditions before embarking on a new development will wait forever); (2) there is always something that can be done to help (because there are a lot of things that can go wrong there are a lot of options for improvement); (3) perfection is not necessary (when enough of the most-needed things have been done, movement will ensue).

The problem for application is to spot the things that most need to be done; that means examination of the situation. A schedule of questions you may find worth asking in such an examination is set out following. It is based on frameworks suggested earlier, but it contains space for you to enter the questions which your experience tells you are also significant factors in helping and hindering change.

Use it, preferably with colleagues, to diagnose readiness for change in relation to the community-linked innovation with which you are concerned.

Diagnosis

Name of programme

Intention and description

The place

Change does not occur in a vacuum. There is a 'context' which has a 'climate'. The context is the organization and/or a network of contacts, its climates are features which tend to support or suppress the suggested change.

Boundary maintenance: is it more or less closed
or open to influences from outside?

             closed   open

Cross-communication: is what is happening in some departments or sections known about and influential in others?

_____

limited   extensive

Decision making: is decision making shared widely; is it known who makes what decision — so they can be approached and influenced?

_____

inaccessible   accessible

Resourcing: what is the time, money, materials, equipment, situation?

_____

tight   slack

What else? [. . .]

_____

_____

_____

The action

Some suggestions for action will be more acceptable than others. Any presentation of a programme of action will have features which tend to give it more or less chance of being taken up.

Common ground: is what is being suggested something which corresponds with preoccupations and intentions in the organization?

_____

low   high

Clarity: do people properly understand what is being suggested?

_____

vague   clear

What else? [. . .]

_____

_____

_____

The promoters

Few changes just happen; usually, one or more persons acts to promote the change. The way such people go about influencing others makes a difference to its chances.

Style: are a variety of methods and styles for persuading, involving and helping others used?

_____

rigid   varied

Communication: is everybody told the same thing, or is what is said tailored to meet the interests of different people?

_____

unnegotiated   negotiated

Social skill: how much personal contact is there so that people can see, hear, recognize and respond to what is being promoted?

_____

impersonal   personal

Influence management: is there flexibility on when to be bold and when to be cautious?

_____

habitual   flexible

What else? [. . .]

_____

_____

The users

People will be involved in the sense that they will be expected to do something new or different. These users of the proposed action will influence its impact.

Understanding: have they taken on board the why? what? and how? of what is being proposed?

_____

no   yes

Resources: can they offer the kind of time, material and skill which is needed?

_____

unmatched   matched

Attitude: do they want to be involved in the
action?

———————————————————

negative   positive

Participation: can they make suggestions for
implementing the action which can be adopted?

———————————————————

not theirs   theirs

What else? [. . .]

———————————————————

———————————————————

The clients

Somebody is expected to gain from the change. These are the clients. They are usually
— but not necessarily — the students in the school, college or training programme. They
will make a difference to its impact.

Preparedness: do they know what is available,
what to expect and can they get ready to gain
what they need from it?

———————————————————

unprepared   prepared

Relatedness: can they relate it to their needs?

———————————————————

irrelevant   relevant

Reflectiveness: do they know what they can get
from it and can they translate it into their own
knowledge, decisions and actions?

———————————————————

no chance   every chance

What else? [. . .]

———————————————————

———————————————————

———————————————————

Chance

Sometimes it is what nobody could have anticipated that turns out to be the critical factor
in the progress of chance. Such chance events can be both an obstruction and an opportunity. Say what and which.

Critical incidents

obstruction	opportunity
obstruction	opportunity
obstruction	opportunity

New actions that can be taken now

By whom? why? what? and how?

What can you do to help? With what priority?

1

2

3

4

The chapter has been designed to bring you to the point where you have identified something you can do to advance some community-linked innovation with which you are concerned. The remainder of the book is given to a more detailed examination of the first five factors for change just mentioned (Table 2.2). Who but you can know about the chance events? It is possible that whatever they are they have something to do with one of the five factors. There is no special order in which the chapters are to be examined. It is up to you to decide what you want to examine next.

TABLE 2.2   Factors examined in detail in later chapters

Factor	Examined in
The place	Chapter 3: Networks and bureaucracies
The action	Chapter 4: Finding common ground
The promoter	Chapter 5: Clout and wisdom
The users	Chapter 7: Users, contributors and audiences
The clients	Chapter 6: Learning from an experience base

CHAPTER 3

NETWORKS AND BUREAUCRACIES

In this chapter the following are examined critically:

- signs of organizational openness to colleague- and community-linked change, and contrary signs
- what costs and benefits there are in community-linked networking
- examples of action that rely on colleague and community links
- a method for tapping network resources.

Schooling is, so to speak, between every kind of devil and every kind of deep blue sea. Everybody has an interest in what schooling does. Most people have vivid memories of what schooling did, and didn't do, for them. Few have no view on the relevance of schooling to their experience and to any interest with which they are now identified.

Pre-vocational education relates what happens inside schooling to experience and interests outside. It therefore threatens to invade what professional educators might take to be 'their' subject, department, school, college or programme. Exposure is destabilizing, eroding the bases of anticipation, preparation and ownership of work in schooling.

A reaction to exposure is the development of a protective shield. It has been a long time since schools sported a 'parents not admitted beyond this point' sign. But protective measures can take more subtle forms, communicating unease about whether and why outsiders should have any influence here. Even colleagues, in outfits like the careers service, the school psychological service and the LEA advisory team, have been known to experience nervousness about entering a school or college. People in one part of an organization have been known to experience difficulty in getting colleagues in another part to open up to the possibility of shared action.

Outside pressure on what happens in schooling, to understate the case, is not diminishing. It will not therefore be surprising to find that schooling maintains, however subtly, its capacity to control who and what is franchised to influence it and who or what is not. The maintenance of the shield can absorb a large part of the organization's energies and become a stable part of its procedures.

Pre-vocational change does not occur in a vacuum. The organization will have a context and climate which will make a difference to whatever proposals for change are to be made. In this chapter attention is paid to the organizational context and climate for change by identifying the characteristics of what are called bureaucracy and networking in organizations. But it does not applaud the virtues of networkings unconditionally; most organizations have, and need, both types of feature. To begin with you are invited to inquire into an organization known to you. This might be a school, college, training programme or community-linked network of people already sharing action.

ACTIVITY

LINKS AND BOUNDARIES

The activity is based on a checklist of characteristics of an organization which appear to be change promoting. It can be used for a personal review of the situation, but is better used as a discussion tool with colleagues. The checklist is in four parts:

(1) Boundary maintenance; can the organization be influenced from outside?
(2) Cross-communication; is what is happening in one part influenced by what is happening elsewhere in the organization?
(3) Decision making; is decision making visible, accessible and dispersed in the organization.
(4) Resourcing; can resource slack be found to support and accommodate new activity?

Ask in what respects, and to what degree, the response to any of the items below is 'yes'. Write down that response, and the evidence to support it. In general, the more evidence you can find for saying 'yes', the more open the organization appears to be to the possibility of change.

Boundary maintenance

There are regular signposting, reception and hospitality provisions for outsiders.

There is plain language description, explanation and news of what is happening, available to outsiders.

You meet outsiders in the organization — and they are treated as though they belong there.

Communication with outsiders includes asking them for their views as well as promoting the organization's views.

Action is not arbitrated by an organization-based range of criteria; each possible action is examined in the light of a wide range of arguments taken from outside as well as inside.

Members who have something to contribute from outside their specialisms are encouraged to do so.

Students contribute to the running of the organization — they are not just clients, but active members in the planning and running of the outfit.

Outsiders contribute to the running of the organization — not just as clients, but as active members in the planning and running of the outfit.

There is no 'job-done' syndrome — members see readily how their work can be extended so that people feel that the job will never be done completely.

Also [. . .].

Cross-communication

Visitors can find, specifically, who they want to meet without having to go through the hierarchy first.

Members plan and review with each other what they are doing — they know what is happening in other parts of the organization and can consult with each other about it.

Interdepartmental teaching or task teams are established.

Members regard the total student population as their concern; particular groups do not concern themselves with particular groups of students exclusively.

There is a variety of such groups forming, working and delivering products to the organization — maximizing interdepartmental thought and action in the life of the organization.

There are some aspects of activity which are regarded as all members' responsibility — whatever their specialisms.

Members are aware of colleagues' different views on the work of the organization; if there is conflict it is acknowledged and confronted — between individuals and across departmental lines.

If one member's or department's valid idea for new action is blocked by lack of resources, then it is conceivable that other members and departments will want to share in the action.

Also [. . .].

Decision making

Members of the organization are expected to achieve their roles by their own ingenuity, imagination and interests; they are not expected slavishly to follow roles assigned to them.

When new members are recruited they are expected to make suggestions about how the role might be developed; they are not expected just to do what their predecessors did.

Decision makers are accessible to approaches from any member who wants to canvass a particular point of view.

Everybody knows what sorts of decisions are made by whom.

Decisions are not first announced after they have been made; they are canvassed in advance, there is discussion and members' views are put forward.

Specific decision making, planning and recommendatory tasks are assigned to groups which take and sift evidence and arrive at recommendations.

Decision making, planning and recommendatory groups are recruited from all levels in the structure.

People who make decisions about new activity are accountable to the people who are required to implement new activity.

As a new activity is allowed to 'bed down' in the operation of the organization, the people involved are given time to review it, point out faults for correction, suggest redesigns and become clear about how and why they are being asked to work in a different way.

Also [. . .].

Resourcing

The employing authority has established salary scales and structures at a level sufficiently attractive to recruit people into the work who are able to identify needs for change and have the abilities and time needed to implement it.

The employing authority has provided sufficiently for the plant, equipment and staff development required to negotiate needed changes successfully.

The organization has developed an idea for new action which has qualified for funding in one of the government's current schemes for education development.

There is a contingency fund to which any promoter of a new activity can apply for resourcing.

The distribution of time, material and equipment can be altered to permit the implementation of a suggestion for new activity.

When a suggestion for new activity is made members are more likely to ask how the resources can be found than to argue that it cannot be done because of lack of resources.

When a new activity is being developed it is possible to count on a degree of goodwill and voluntarism for the extra work and effort it involves.

People do not refuse to consider new activity solely on the grounds that it is not in their job descriptions or contracts.

There are links with people and organizations outside which are capable of acquiring new resources.

Also [. . .].

INPUT

BASES FOR ACTION

All organizations (such as commercial and industrial firms, cooperatives, communes, churches, clubs, families, schools, colleges and the careers service) combine some characteristics of both bureaucracy (column 2 of the schemes following) and network (column 3). Few are wholly of one type, although most tend in one direction or the other. On the whole a networking basis for action is more favourable to adaptiveness and to community-linked activity. But it also has its disadvantages.

BOUNDARY MAINTENANCE

Bureaucratic organizations embody a clear sense of what is inside and what is outside the organization, and a concomitant belief in the adequacy of its own authority and resources. Networking organizations blur the distinction between what is inside and outside.

Function and clientele may be [. . .]	[. . .] defined firmly and relatively fixed.	[. . .] defined loosely and extendable.
Roles may be [. . .]	[. . .] assigned by the organization; people know what is expected of them.	[. . .] achieved by participants; people can invent their own roles.
Information about what is going on may be [. . .]	[. . .] held internally.	[. . .] dispersed.
Rationales and resources for action may be [. . .]	[. . .] generated internally.	[. . .] trawled from outside-the-organization sources.

CROSS-COMMUNICATION

Bureaucratic organizations rely on consensual agreements that each department is responsible for, and in control of, its own actions; and a concomitant sense that other departments' actions and clientele are their own responsibilities. Networking organizations blur the distinctions between departments, seeking to cross-fertilize and support organization-wide action, with its possibilities for conflict among 'too many cooks'.

Action may be [. . .]	[. . .] planned, developed implemented and reported department-by-department.	[. . .] something which, overall, all participants contribute to, so that people do not feel concerned with one part of the operation exclusively.

Information consultancy resources and support may be [. . .]	[. . .] held within, and sought from, closest colleagues in the organization.	[. . .] shared widely.
Conflict may be [. . .]	[. . .] avoided in consensus building which participants are not expected to oppose.	[. . .] acknowledged, so that concerns and oppositions are confronted.

DECISION MAKING

Bureaucratic organizations are hierarchical, depending on the assumed probity of a small number of people who make all the major decisions for policy and strategy in the organization. Networking organizations are in a perpetual state of reviewing decision making in all parts of the organization.

Decision may be located [. . .]	[. . .] with a small number of bosses.	[. . .] in a dispersed web of participants.
Its visibility may be [. . .]	[. . .] low; other people do not know when, where and — even by whom — decisions are made.	[. . .] high; everybody knows what is going on and who is involved.
Its procedure may be [. . .]	[. . .] firm and fixed — even irreversible.	[. . .] phased, taking account of alternatives, consultations and modified where required.
Accountability may be [. . .]	[. . .] required by decision makers of users.	[. . .] required of decision makers by users.
Predictability may be [. . .]	[. . .] easier; there are rules, precedents, terms of reference, which are used to justify decisions.	[. . .] harder; decision making is opportunistic in changing situations.

RESOURCING

Bureaucratic organizations make the probability of any new action being adopted dependent on the availability of resources; resource availability is one of the first questions to be asked. Networking organizations set out to realign resource allocations and beg, borrow and, in some cases, steal resources to make what seems desirable possible.

New action [...]	[...] generally, increases pressure on resources.	[...] is accompanied by action to get new resources.
Resources are conceived [...]	[...] in terms of cash value, budgets and contracted allocations.	[...] as people, skills, materials, sites, which can be volunteered and bartered as well as cash budgetted.
Allocations are [...]	[...] based departmentally.	[...] transferred and shared between departments.

EXAMPLES

LINKING STRUCTURES

On the following pages are accounts of activity which rely on the use of fewer bureaucratic and more networking procedures. They are analysed, along with all the other examples cited in this book, in Table 3.1. This shows where the accounts pay attention to the features mentioned in this chapter: boundary maintenance, cross-communication, decision making and resourcing. Also, another feature is taken into consideration, here called 'type of attachment'.

Some community-linked activity, such as Education Work Councils (C1), are based on an organization which has been designed wholly for this purpose. They are classified in the analysis as *free standing*. Others, such as Manningham Careers and Educational Advice Centre and Outreach Workers (C3), have their roots in an existing structure, with which they retain links. But they have been developed in a more-or-less free-standing way to pursue community-linked activity. These are classified as *emergent*. Yet others, such as the Community Contacts Directory (C2), have been developed wholly within an existing organization, with a context and climate which may or may not be preoccupied with community links, and which has whatever combination of bureaucratic and networking sympathies and procedures there may be. These are classified as *rooted*.

The codes refer to accounts to be found in other chapters as follows: A in Chapter 1; B in Chapter 2; D in Chapter 4; F in Chapter 7.

TABLE 3.1   Linking structures: examples of types and features of organization of attachment

Features	Type of attachment		
	Free standing	Emergent	Rooted
Boundary maintenance	A2, A5, C1, F1	A3, A4, B2, C3, F2	A1, A6, A7, B1, C2, D1, D3, F3
Cross-communication	A5, C1	A3, A4, B2, C3	A6, B1, C2, D1, D2, D3, F3
Decision making	A5, C1, F1	A3, A4, B2, C3, F2	A6, A7, B1, C2, D1, D3
Resourcing	A2, A5, C1	A3, A4, B2, C3, F2	A7, C2, D1

C1   Education Work Councils

EWCs are free-standing organizations in their own communities; they are not adjuncts of education authorities, schools, colleges or any of their other constituent organizations. Their concern is 'relying on local community initiative to ferry people across the gap between education and employment' and to 'infuse the coming-of-age process with knowledge and experience available in the broader community'. Their memberships, of around 40 persons, comprise 'senior officials' from local government, commercial and industrial organizations, churches, social service agencies, trade unions, schools, colleges and parents associations. They set out to be 'credible' and 'neutral', to whom any constituent organization or community group can turn for help. They are concerned with school and college curricula, but they also address the needs of other client groups, such as working women and the elderly in the community. The National Institute of Work and Learning in Washington DC affiliates EWCs, and supports their action with ideas, promotion, literature, consultancy and — for a time — money from federal funding.

Boundary maintenance

The argument is for 'removing barriers'. Any organization which becomes a constituent of an EWC exposes itself to outside influence. Part of the rationale for EWCs is that schools and colleges, in particular, have allowed arbitrary splits to be fixed between themselves and adult and working life and that they also arbitrarily split the careers of people into phases to be devoted first to 'education' and then to 'work'. A frequent first action of EWCs is to enquire into the needs of local client groups, local labour economic trends or the local impact of labour laws; this information is used to influence decision making in the constituent organizations. 'Return and learn' and experience-based schemes form prominent parts of EWCs' influence on schools and colleges.

Cross-communication

Making what is happening visible within and between the constituent organizations is an important part of EWCs' work. They frequently develop directories of available resources, facilities and programmes so that members of one part of the action can co-ordinate with others. Seminars and workshops are established in which, for example, business people infuse school curricula with knowledge and materials from the commercial world. But they tend to avoid conflict, by postponing 'hot' issues. They are argued by their advocates to be 'consensus-building' operations.

Decision making

The whole council is involved in the identification of needs, objectives, resources, preferred implementation and outcomes of activity. Constituent organizations — having become members — negate the point of the council if they arbitrarily resist its influence. For example, an EWC survey of student interests and aspirations in one area leads to the drafting of career and vocational education proposals for district schools by the school superintendent. Advocates of EWCs argue that its members should be 'power brokers' from within the constituent organizations with sufficient position and leverage to be able to get the thrust of its thinking implemented in their organizations. Those same advocates, however, resist any attempts by decision making at higher levels to control community-based EWCs; it is argued that state legislation to support EWC activity should not be undertaken.

Resourcing

Councils seek voluntary allocations of space and facilities from constituent organizations, for such activities as work-experience programmes. Some EWCs ask for membership contributions from constituent organizations. As they become stronger and more prominent they also seek government funding. Some EWCs have attracted sufficient resources to be able to establish a full-time executive office.

Advocates of EWCs argue that they do not exist primarily to foster any particular kind of development, but development which is identified to be appropriate to the needs of the communities in which they are set. The emphasis is therefore on the value of the adaptive process rather than on the advocacy of any particular 'angle' (such as education-for-industry). However, although they are argued to be consensus-building organizations, they do become politicized by constituent interests, dominant voices 'hijack' some EWCs for their own purposes.

Sources: Wirtz, 1975; Law, 1982.

C2   Community Contacts Directory

The directory is a card-index system containing contact information about people in the neighbourhood of the school who have agreed to meet students informally and, at a time that can be arranged easily, to talk with them about their experience in some part of the working life of the community. The cards are indexed much as conventional careers literature is indexed. The cards and the contacts they note are a resource in the careers interviewing programme of the school.

Boundary maintenance

The directory is an acknowledgement that the school does not contain all the resources needed to anticipate and prepare students for participation in working life in the community. It 'franchises' people in the neighbourhood to participate in the education of students, on the basis of their personal authority as members of the community's working life. These are — for the most part — not 'official' representatives of industry and commerce, but people in day-to-day contact with all aspects of working life. Some contacts are — at first — puzzled by the invitation to participate, wondering what they have to offer to what the school and the Careers Service already provide. The coordinator points out that they have authentic knowledge of what it is like to be in the community's work environments, and schooling needs this knowledge.

Cross-communication

The existence of the directory is advertised widely in the school through the already available methods for making staff, parents and students aware of what is going on. 'Pastoral' and 'guidance' functions are claimed to be responsibilities of all teachers. Any teacher can refer students to the directory. Pastoral teachers participate in the careers interviewing programme of the school and the directory is made available to them specifically.

Decision making

Decision making arises from a continuous process of consultation, monitoring and review. The guidance coordinator recruits members of the network. A variety of formal and informal methods for meeting potential members of the network are used; parents evenings, chance encounters and specifically arranged meetings for local people in village pubs, all form part of the canvassing and recruiting process. Other members of staff are encouraged to suggest possible contacts. Contacts are reported to be nervous, at first, about offering help to students; the coordinator talks with them about what they can and cannot reasonably be expected to do to help students. The time and place of meeting is controlled by the contacts and students. Contacts with people of particular interest to them are arranged by the students, following their interview. The coordinator informally follows up students who have made a contact to monitor its usefulness to them.

Resourcing

The operation is resourced wholly from what people are prepared to offer the programme; no additional time, provision or money has been sought. The operation needs time to get started but, once in operation, can be maintained, updated and monitored within reasonable resource limits.

Networking raises the possibility that some students will eventually make a contact which — in one sense or another — will prove harmful. The coordinator monitors with this possibility in mind. Doubtful contacts are removed from the directory. Networking also present the possibility of extension to a wide variety of working roles — including those outside paid employment. There is no reason, either, why students should not be involved in canvassing, negotiating and updating entries to the directory.

Source: Anon.

C3   Manningham Careers and Educational Advice Centre and Outreach Workers

The centre is located, in a former church, by the Bradford Careers Service in an inner-city area with high unemployment. Outreach workers are part of the service's general strategy. Both are intended to contact people who do not visit main service offices. Careers service personnel seek to cooperate with local people on the improvement of their life chances; that concern extends to cultural and recreational activities as well as to job seeking.

Boundary maintenance

The centre is designed to take careers officers out of the role of 'bureaucratic specialist' and to put some of them into an 'outreach' role. This means that they consult and liaise with local groups about what sorts of services should be provided, they develop plain language material explaining what is available, they jig and staff the centre to encourage informal 'drop in' visits, they visit clients in their homes — working with families as well as individuals, they respond to requests to set up part of the service in other organization's premises (such as mosques), and they recruit a network of 'jobmates' to help local young people who need more opportunity to see at first hand what is happening in the adult and working life of the neighbourhood.

Cross-communication

Careers officers maintain contacts with other parts of local authority provision. Outreach workers liaise closely with youth workers. The service sees itself as a contact to make other parts of the 'bureaucracy' more comprehending of, and accessible to, their clientele. Officers accept invitations to participate in staff development programmes for workers in other parts of the local authority's services. They must, at times, negotiate with their employing authority on behalf of their clients. For example, recommendations for land clearance and reclamation have been passed to the city council and have been amalgamated into its 'Operation Eyesore' programme.

Decision making

Careers officers see themselves as helpers who can suggest new developments, but who must not impose them. It is a matter of sensing needs rather than imposing provisions. They report that representatives of local ethnic groups have sought contact with them to work out what can best be done for local people. The centre's officers can find themselves — at times — at the centre of conflicts.

Resourcing

The service has bid for additional government and community programme funding successfully. The work is considerably more time consuming than conventional careers service work. It calls on considerable personal resources from its workers.

Caller traffic to the centre is reported to have increased steadily. An early 1-year monitoring exercise showed that the proportion of young unemployed had fallen from 20 per cent of the district total to 7 per cent (the population of the neighbourhood represents 8 per cent of the district). Like all forms of networking such outreach work can be extended readily to take account of opportunities outside paid employment. But it calls on resilience in its workers, who — at times — will be negotiating not only with local groups but also with their own employing authority. Not all communities can be recognized and served in this way — some, such as some rural communities, are much more diffuse.

Source: Howden, 1985.

EXPLORATION

SECOND THOUGHTS ON NETWORKING

BOUNDARIES AND LINKS

Much of the previous analysis of bureaucracy and network can be traced back to Durkheim, who characterized societies as tending toward what he called 'mechanical' or 'organic' cohesion (cited in Giddens, 1972).

A society high on mechanical cohesion depends on the similarity of beliefs held by its members. Those beliefs are crystallized into a detailed, consensual and, eventually, statutory regulation of conduct. Individuals are therefore led not to expect conflict with others. Nor are they encouraged to identify any conflict between self and role. They accept the assignment to them of their roles. Such a society can lose much of its membership without serious damage to its continuity; its members have a very clear sense of who and what is inside, and acceptable, and what is outside, and unacceptable, to the group.

A society high on organic cohesion depends on the differences between its members. Conflict is part of the stuff of which society is made. It deals with conflict in terms of civil and lateral, rather than statutory and regulated, action. Members expect to be able to achieve new roles. The society therefore becomes more complex and diverse; correspondingly, it becomes more difficult to determine who and what is inside and who and what is outside. There is more tolerance for deviance.

Durkheim's analysis is capable of application to organizations such as firms and schools. One application refers to schools organized on more 'closed' or 'open' lines (Bernstein, 1967, 1971).

The trend, Bernstein argued, is away from closed schools. These control behaviour by institutional (even ritualistic) rather than personal means, carrying the message 'the rules here do not permit the kind of behaviour' rather than 'I don't like what you are doing'. They have a few simply defined roles; there will be a small number of management roles and teacher roles will be undiversified into such specialisms as guidance and counselling. They are resistant to outside influence; the views of parents and the impact of 'alternative' cultures will not be priorities. Curriculum will be tightly framed; a clear boundary is set between what may and what may not be taught. Also, it will be classified tightly; clear boundaries are set between subjects, pre-empting cross-curricular activity. Roles are assigned to teachers, de-emphasizing their individuality; when a teacher is replaced the newcomer will be expected to do much what her or his predecessor did. Teachers are not expected to introduce experience from outside their specialist disciplines.

The trend, it was argued, is toward open schools, where behaviour is developed by relationships which recognize subtle differences between individuals. The positions of teachers and students are fixed less rigidly and take account of a wider range of possibilities; simple streaming or banding of students is less likely. Teachers are less isolated from each other; teams are formed and re-formed for a variety of purposes. There is less concern with purity of what schooling does; curriculum is framed and classified less tightly. Teachers are able to develop their own conceptions of role and to introduce material which was not formerly thought to be part of the curriculum. Bernstein sees all of this as highly functional in terms of the need for adaptiveness on the part of schools.

Such analyses have value beyond keeping academic sociologists out of worse mischief. They identify three franchises to extend the network of resources available to pre-vocational education.

FIRST FRANCHISE
The first franchise invites links with the adult experience of workers in the education

system. It invites them to invade what they do in their work with what they have learned elsewhere. Staff in the Manningham Centre (**C3**) call on more skills and experience than a conventional role description of careers officers suggests; the inclusion of teachers in the Community Contacts Directory (**C2**), on the basis of experience and interests outside their subjects, would also be an example of such a franchise. Teachers know more than the formality of schooling invites them to use. They have previous and outside experience as adults which can be useful to students.

In the development of a new syllabus on adult working life at 'Dane Park' School, described in detail later in this book (**F3**), there is disagreement about how much of their personal experience and attitudes should be disclosed to students. It comes to a dilemma between 'neutral chairperson' and 'disclosing adult'. Disclosing adult does not imply making ex-cathedra statements from an authoritarian pedestal; it means letting students know how this particular adult, on the basis of his or her particular experience, sees it. The 'Dane Park' group is unable to reach consensus on the issue. Those who argue for it argue on the grounds that it will promote more adult–adult relations between students and teachers.

The teachers who consult with students on their own Community Newspaper, reported later (**D3**), are also offering to change the relation between students and teachers, along the lines 'this is how I — a partner with you — see it'.

Actually, most teachers do, informally anyway, bring their outside interests into the classroom. It can prove to be of more interest and relevance to students than the material of the pure curriculum. The role is 'adults-who-happen-to-be-teachers'.

SECOND FRANCHISE

The second franchise invites more links between the elements in the existing system. It assumes that the pre-vocational needs of students will not be met by one, or even a few, departments or sections in any organization. It assumes that cross-organization action is necessary; that interdepartmental cooperation will occur. The second franchise requires that the boundaries between the subjects and departments of schooling can be made more permeable, linking more of what is happening in schooling to the pre-vocational needs of students.

The principle applies not only to schools and colleges. The Manningham Centre's work in negotiating with and feeding back to other departments in the local authority is an example (**C3**), as is the inclusion of a range of local institutions in the internal organization of Education Work Councils (**C1**). The careers coordinator of the Community Contacts Directory (**C2**) uses the directory to support pastoral-care staff in their roles in pre-vocational help offered to students.

THIRD FRANCHISE

The third franchise offers more links between what happens inside and people outside the existing system. The boundary between schooling and the outside world is made more permeable. This is the most radical form of franchising, not just to the 'other' experience of teachers, nor just to 'other' teachers who were not involved formerly, but to adults-other-than-teachers in all the roles described in Chapter 1.

The recruitment of adults-other-than-teachers to the Community Contacts Directory is a further example (**C2**), as is the recruitment of job mates and the entry into consultation with neighbourhood contacts in the Manningham Centre (**C3**).

PRE-VOCATIONAL EDUCATION: FOR ATTACHMENTS AND ALTERNATIVES?

Franchising can extend curriculum and it can diversify its use. Extension means the attachment of students to more material from the adult working life of their community. That is the intention at 'Dane Park' (**F3**), to develop a new syllabus which will have material in it about industry, trades unions, social and life skills and so on. Diversifying means infusing more perspectives into the existing curriculum. That is the intention at Crofton School (**A1**), where existing activity in music is diversified to take account, among other things, of the pre-vocational planning of musicians among its students.

A theoretical analysis of life chances distinguishes between the importance of what are called 'ligatures' and 'options' (Dahrendorf, 1979). Ligatures are attachments; options are alternatives. The strengthening of both, Dahrendorf argues, is necessary to the improvement of life chances.

Ligatures maintain continuities, they fasten people to the sustained structures of their experience in space and time, nation and history, generation and community, family and society. This is the stuff of the transmitted curriculum. Curriculum transmission is a major means by which we seek to attach our people to society; to give them a sense of the cultural soil on which they stand. So is work, or, at least, paid employment. To have paid employment is to have connection with the society in which membership is thereby held.

The strengthening of ligatures is sought by programmes described here. At Manningham (**C3**) there is an explicit intention to use the centre as a means of reinforcing local people in their cultural identities. It is intended also that the centre will be a route to other parts of the local authority's bureaucracy (in the sense that it is hoped that, once they have visited the centre, clients will be prepared to use other services of the local authority). An intention of the Community Contacts Directory (**C2**) is to make the working lives of ordinary people in the mainstream life of the neighbourhood more visible to young men and women.

Options create new variations on the underlying structures of experience, acknowledging that people can make alternative histories, communities, families, ways of working and curricula. Schooling that invites the diversified use of curriculum material enlarges options. At Manningham they deliberately encourage development of a range of social, leisure and alternative working roles. The Community Contacts Directory could be adapted to include such purposes readily. All teachers do both things: they transmit curriculum and they invite alternative responses to it. But teachers vary with regard to the degree of emphasis they give to transmission of ligatures and invitations to options.

An enquiry into the attitudes of secondary-school teachers engaged in counselling and guidance work suggests that a major consideration in resolving their working dilemmas is a sense for the existing structure of schooling. A spectrum of value-laden attitudes to that structure emerged (Law, 1977a). Some want to work through the system, accepting the assignment to them of their roles, and remaining loyal to the current objectives of schooling. They are higher on 'system orientation', emphasizing the importance of maintaining attachments between their work and the school's current way of working. Others, lower on system orientation, prefer to achieve roles which have some independence from existing procedures and beliefs, are prepared to tolerate conflicts with colleagues on how their counselling and guidance work should be done and emphasize the need to provide alternatives to what schooling currently offers.

The improvement of life chances, Dahrendorf argues, is a function of both ligatures and options, much as the area of a field is a function of both its breadth and length. Stronger anchorages improve life chances, so do larger possibilities for varying them; that would give the people of Manningham a shot with the bureaucracy, and another with the alternative activities springing up in the district.

Curriculum can be made to offer more life chances by extending it to the right, beyond A (Figure 3.1). That means that, in addition to learning (say) about history, students learn about work, family or social and life skills in separate subjects on the timetable. More material to cram in.

Careers education became a new subject on the timetable and, at the beginning, was taught as though it were an academic subject with its own body of knowledge, concepts and skills. Teachers who have a sense of the purity of the concepts, knowledge, skills and attitudes contained by the existing curriculum resist it as an intrusion. Teachers who have a sense of the value of creating options resist it as merely replicating more of an already too-limited outside world, inside schooling.

Curriculum can be made to offer more life chances by applying it to a wider range of options, toward B (Figure 3.1). History is taught as the history of work, of family or of how people solve their interpersonal and political problems in a way which relates to the

FIGURE 3.1   Extension of curriculum to offer more life chances

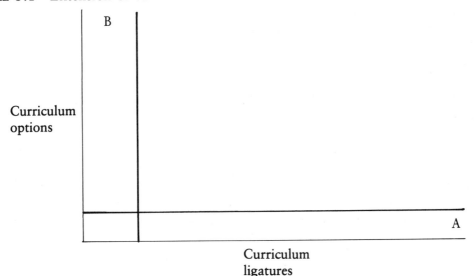

problems and decisions that students must solve and make in their own lives. It includes more opportunities for students to take the concepts, skills and attitudes contained within any subject, and to apply and reapply them to alternatives. Teachers' own outside experience shows how it can be reapplied, colleagues involved in cross-curricular projects cross-fertilize reapplication and the involvement in those projects of adults-other-than-teachers more so. There is no subject on the timetable that has proved incapable of being applied to the pre-vocational needs of students.

It means that attention should be paid to the use that students make of the material. That is what has happened to careers education. Its workers have become more interested in its processes than in trying to identify its discrete content. In parallel with that shift of emphasis, there is the realization that any piece of existing curriculum material can be applied to the careers-development needs of students. There are more options in existing curriculum than have been realized. The argument is not so much for more curriculum material, but for the more varied use of the material we already have.

BASES OF OPERATION

The network-based reapplication of schooling is destabilizing. Bernstein (1967) warns against the possibility that open schools will leave students (and, presumably, teachers) with little recognizable sense of what is required of them. Dahrendorf (1979) suggests that it is a requirement for the creative pursuit of options that there is already a sufficiently secure level attachment.

People need order, some more than others. The study of counselling and guidance attitudes (Law, 1978) was extended to show that system orientation is personality related: teachers who are prepared to risk independence of the system and conflict with colleagues, are people who, in general, take up an inner-directed stance on decision making; they seem to be equipped with personal 'gyroscopes' which keep them on their courses, despite the ambiguities, buffetings and set-backs of experience. However, system orientation is distributed normally; most people take a middle position. Thoroughgoing inner directedness is a minority phenomenon; most people have some degree of 'other-directed' need for stable expectations and cues concerning what they will do.

Reports of the work at Manningham (C3) refer to the need for considerable personal resources of resilience in carrying out that work. The careers coordinator risking the franchising of adults-other-than-teachers through the Community Contacts Directory (C2), none the less, keeps a careful eye on its effects and removes any risky contacts.

The head of City-as-school (A2) reports difficulties with a careful education board's forward-planning requirements. It wants management-by-objectives declared in advance, but the resources of the school are community based and in a perpetual state of interruption by losses and gains of contacts: 'everything is an interruption of everything else'. It is not predictable management-by-objectives, but 'seat-of-pants' management-by-opportunity.

Networking activity, which pursues alternatives, opens boundaries, sullies purity, diffuses decision making and risks conflict, increases threat. It can be made to sound very attractive, but also it can open itself naively to whatever transient, arbitrary or vested interest happens to be fashionable or dominant. Some Education Work Councils (C1) are 'hijacked', in much the way that teachers, anticipating further replication in schools of the power relations in society-at-large, feared.

The unsullied subject base, free from outside intrusion (where I know what is going on and it is in my control), has attractions which it would be reckless to ignore. Most people to some extent, and some people to a very considerable extent, need to feel that the system is reasonably secure and predictable (that the outfit I show up in for this Monday morning is going to be much like the one I left in last Friday afternoon): a base of operation. There are some networking organizations that do not qualify on this criterion.

The base of operations for a retailer is a shop; however, the concept in schooling cannot be defined so concretely. A base of operations is the minimal establishment of intentions, roles, resources, expectations and discretions necessary for manageable action. It is recognizable and stable, but not necessarily imposed and fixed. Without it there can be no basis for anticipating, planning or accountability. Without it, when people are asked to link, they do not know what it is that they are being asked to link to.

There are examples of three types of base of operation in this book. An analysis appears in the beginning of the examples section in this chapter.

ROOTED

Rooted bases use the existing machinery of the host organization. A great deal of individual and small-group activity by people determined to blaze a trail, with or without hierarchical support, is like this. Work shadowing at Crofton School (A1), the Working Lives Project (A7), the use of the Community Contacts Directory (C2) and the Community Newspaper Project (D3) are examples (at least in the sense that they rely on the stable bureaucratic provisions of the organizations in which they are set). They cannot survive without them. In some cases the contribution of such operations is not only to deliver the goods to the clientele, but also to show the host organization how its own procedures can be adapted to fruitful networking activity.

EMERGENT

Emergent operations detach partly from an originating organization and establish their own parallel bases, which overlap with procedures in the originating organization. The more emergent they are, the more of their own bureaucracy they have established, then the more likely it is that they will survive the closure of the host organization. In the Transition to Working Life Project (A3) a design feature is the establishment of a new and autonomous structure, established across the boundary of the school, but requiring its own reliable allocations of time and resources. At Madeley Court School (B2) an early step in the development of community-linked activity is the establishment of mini-schools attached to the host organization, but with well-defined territories, with their own collections of resources and roles. Both maintain some element of predictable structure for the operation of networking activity.

FREE STANDING

Free-standing operations start from scratch, establishing wholly new machinery. That can be a problem if there is no obvious starting base. One of the difficulties acknowledged by the proposers of the Post-Youth Training Scheme Partnerships (**A5**) is that, because the responsibility for getting it moving cannot be seen as anybody's in particular, then the danger is that it will be seen as nobody's at all. Yet a prime mover for education work councils in the United States, Wirtz (1975), strongly argues the case for free-standing organization. His argument is that linked activity based inside schools gives too much control to schools. He uses the analogy of the necessity for a bridge to be based firmly on piers at both ends. An education work council is the community-based pier for the bridge. But, without clear dependence on a single host organization these councils prove vulnerable to take over, which is, perhaps, why some show signs of developing bureaucracies of their own (backed by consensus between institutionalized 'power brokers' to whom decision making is restricted, with budgets and salaried secretaries).

It may, in the end, prove necessary to characterize networks as 'symbiotic' parasites on bureaucracies.

ACTION

NEGOTIATING CHANGE

This action involves participants in organization development, identifying possibilities and priorities for action, identifying helps and hindrances to those actions and embarking on the negotiations to maximize what will help and minimize what will hinder. The setting might be a single institution and its partners in the community, a consortium of educational institutions and their partners in the community, members of a department, faculty or section within a school or college and their partners elsewhere.

Also the procedures have been used both as staff-development or training activity. In staff development it is set up as a simulation in which members of the participant group take the various roles in the agreed setting and its network of partners. In organization development the various roles are actually represented in the group and transactions are real not simulated. In staff development the aims are to identify, rehearse and practise the processes of networking. In organization-development activity the aim is to embark on a process of networking.

The procedure assumes that between 20 and 60 people are present, and one person per 20 participants to manage the procedure and enable the process. It engages participants in individual activity, group activity and plenary activity. The whole procedure requires the equivalent of at least 1 day's work. Some phases of activity can be modified or removed, to bring the time required to around 3 hours.

The procedure assumes that the participants know about the setting: the organization and its community, what the needs of students are and what actions are being undertaken currently. Where, in organization-development sessions, such knowledge cannot be assumed it is important to arrange some preliminary stages in which that information can be exchanged. In staff-development sessions it is possible that participants are coming from a number of different organizations. In that case an agreed setting will have to be built, into which this procedure is being introduced. A useful way of doing this is to use a plenary session to build a case study of the setting which represents most of the issues with which participants are concerned. It is possible also to use any of the case-study examples given in this book as a portrayal of the setting into which the simulation is being introduced.

FIRST STAGE: 'WHO, WHAT AND WHY?'

Working individually identify at least one action that should be taken in this setting. On a piece of paper that can later be displayed to the whole group write a 'who, what and why?' sheet. Who do you say is to take the action, what is the action and why should it be undertaken?

SECOND STAGE: 'WHAT DO YOU MAKE OF THIS?'

Working with a stranger show your 'who, what and why?' sheet to your partner. Do not explain it; ask your partner to tell you what your proposal(s) means to him or her. You tell her or him what each of his or her proposals means to you. The point is that your partner will understand your proposal in a way which will be different from what you intended. Discuss and clarify any misunderstandings; consider any new possibilities for the idea that will have emerged. You may want to rewrite your proposal to take that discussion into account.

THIRD STAGE: 'POOLING OF THE IDEAS'

Put all the 'who, what and why?' sheets where everybody can see them. Arrange them so that proposals for action by different groups are together: where the 'who' is school bosses, they go together, where the 'who' is the employers, they go together and so on. Have a look at the ideas, get a feel for what the people in this network have in mind.

FOURTH STAGE: 'TAKE A ROLE'

From the arrangement of the sheets the range of roles which are seen as agents for action will have been identified. The whole group divides into those roles. From now on you will be asked to consider proposals for action from the point of view of the role you find yourself in. A useful procedure is to time a break for now, so that circles of chairs can be arranged to locate each of the role groups to be involved. Each group of chairs is labelled clearly with its role. As people come back they elect their roles on a first-come-first-served basis.

FIFTH STAGE: 'WHAT COMES FIRST?'

In your role group pick up the 'who, what and why?' proposals that are addressed to you. Your task is to consider which, if any, you can take action on. As you take your decisions display the 'adopted' sheets so that the rest of the groups can see them. Any that you do not adopt should be returned to the pool. You can also adopt any from the pool which, although they were not addressed to you, you decide that you can take action on. You may want to adapt or combine proposals before you decide to adopt them; you may want to make new proposals for action. All these options are open to you: adopt, adapt, combine, discard, design. If there is a proposal that you do not understand draw attention to it until the author comes and explains it to you. On your final display of adopted proposals put the high priority ones at the top and arrange the others in order underneath.

SIXTH STAGE: 'WHY THIS AND NOT THAT?'

Have a look at how the various role groups have adapted suggestions and ordered their priorities; have a look at what has not been adopted and is still in the pool. In whole-group exchange challenge, question or support any of the decisions that have been made. You may be able to begin to see why certain kinds of action are being accepted and why others are not. You may be able to see it, but you are not obliged to agree to it. In any event it will do no harm to point out what you see.

SEVENTH STAGE: 'NEGOTIATION OF ACTION'

Back in your role group reconsider your high-priority actions. It's not too late to change. On the basis of what are now your priorities, your task now is to identify who else in the room you need to communicate with to carry things forward. Decide what you want to say to whom. Agree the wording and write it out on a memo slip. Send memos through the post office. You will also receive messages, replies to which you will need to consider, agree and write. Replies also go through the post office. The number of messages available to each group will depend on how much time is available. A rough-and-ready guide is one message for each 10 min of time available to this phase. The availability of messages can be controlled by issuing a fixed number of memo forms to each group. Answer forms (more conveniently printed on a different coloured paper) can be made available as needed. (The post office is a central spot where the managing and enabling staff will receive and distribute messages and have a chance to see what is being said.) It can be useful also to make a sociogram-type display of all messages and replies. The resulting display has boxes representing each role group (putting 'bosses' in the middle usually eases the graphics because they receive a lot of messages). Between the boxes are lines and arrows indicating the travel of messages, in one colour, and replies, in another. Showing the sociogram (with numbers of each box indicating total messages sent and total received) at the end of the transactions can identify which groups have been central and which marginal and raises the question 'why?'.

EIGHTH STAGE: 'WHERE DO WE GO FROM HERE?'

Stay in your role group. This procedure has been designed to: identify, refine and develop some proposals for action; gain and, if necessary, challenge a sense of what priority is being given to them by the group as a whole; and embark on a process of negotiation between the groups to be involved. That will have raised all kinds of issues on which you will want to speak. Not least among them may be negotiations which have ground to a halt in writing, but may be capable of being continued orally.

What happens here cannot, of course, be scripted by any designed procedure. In organization-development activity the outcomes are, most usefully, contracted agreements between partners in the network concerning action which will be undertaken in the ensuing days and weeks. The public writing and displaying of such undertakings may be a possible endpoint and, if it is possible, will certainly be useful. In staff-development activity the wash-up might be less specific to a known institution. Some enablers to discussion may find some of the material set out elsewhere in this book useful as handout resources to identify and inform the issues for negotiation of change in organizations brought up by participants.

CHAPTER 4

FINDING COMMON GROUND

In this chapter the following are examined critically:

- the variety of intentions infused into cross-curricular community-linked schooling
- a needs-based analysis of curriculum objectives
- how young adults develop alternative career strategies to meet their needs
- how schooling can diagnose its pre-vocational effort.

Curriculum answers the questions 'what sorts of problems do we want our people to be able to solve?' and 'what sorts of decisions do we want them to be able to make?'.

The answers can be colour coded. Education for self-employment, enterprise, competitiveness and employable capability is, for some anyway, ominously blue. Programmes that emphasize the value of voluntary work, community service, leisure pursuits (often in the arts and crafts and really healthy sports), conservation, reclamation, urban renewal and sensitivity training may be seen, by others, as innocently green. While attention paid to dealing with the DHSS, communes, cooperatives, assertiveness training and right to work action might be thought, by yet others, to be dangerously red. It can make a stunning variation in the pre-vocational colouration to be found between Adam Smith Associates (Training) Ltd., Bourneville Community School and the Harry Pollitt Drop-in Centre.

In what we like to think is still a democratic and pluralistic society, the problems we want our people to be able to solve and the decisions we want them to be able to make should straddle all parts of the spectrum. Each curriculum should be like Joseph's coat: of many colours.

Cross-curricular and community-linked education permits diversity. The problem of finding and coordinating that diversity is addressed in this chapter. Not much is learned in schooling that is the property of one subject on any timetable exclusively. This is demonstrable, even where curriculum is classified wholly by subject headings. Say you are a specialist in religious education (but transpose this to whatever your specialism happens to be). Students learn about religion with other teachers and they learn about more than religion with you. Classify your curriculum material in other ways and its shared nature becomes even more visible. The idea that ethnic consciousness, self-awareness, language, social and life skills or aesthetics are the private property of any subject is a fiction which can only be maintained by academic purism and the isolation of specialist teachers in their classrooms.

Neither is much learned in schooling that is learned wholly in school. The idea that it is only teachers who teach is a well-eroded schoolman's myth. Teachers are well aware that every piece of information acquired, concept developed, skill sharpened and attitude applauded depends on what happens beyond the framing of schooling. There are specialists in religion outside school (and our temples, synagogues, mosques and churches are not the only examples). There are also less specialized, but no less insistent, voices for and against religion to be found in the warp and weft of media and neighbourhood life. Students sift, compare, and assign, or do not assign, weight to what is put forward by teachers, on the basis of what they have learned beyond schooling. Residual denials of this reality diagnose bad cases of delusions of grandeur on the part of teachers. Few teachers suffer from the disorder.

It is a design feature of pre-vocational education that these links, between subjects, and between what happens inside and outside school, become a planned part of curriculum development. It raises issues for how broad a spectrum of colouration can be permitted to infuse curriculum, a matter for values. It also raises issues for how possible it is to find any common ground between them, a matter for viability.

ACTIVITY

THE SHARED CURRICULUM

In this activity you are invited to test for the value and viability of such links in any part of the work with which you are concerned currently. It is an extension of the mapping activity at the beginning of Chapter 1, resting on the same analysis of 'inside the organization' versus 'outside the organization' and 'specialist' versus 'non-specialist' contributions (Figure 4.1). It can be extended further into the action for a curriculum audit outlined at the end of this chapter.

Think of a piece of learning, with pre-vocational relevance, that you seek to help students achieve, something that might take between 1 and 4 weeks in your programme. Analyse the contribution to that learning of at least four diverse sources: (1) yourself and immediate colleagues, as specialists in the work; (2) people inside the organization who do not have your specialist commitment to your field (in schooling this is often extracurricular activity); (3) specialist or formal help that is offered from outside the organization (from people who have a commitment to the field similar to your own); (4) outside contacts with no particular specialism or commitment to your field (in schooling work-experience contacts are often like that, although you could include other contacts of a much less formal type).

Make a list of who contributes what in terms of what is done, with what intentions

FIGURE 4.1   Shared curriculum activity

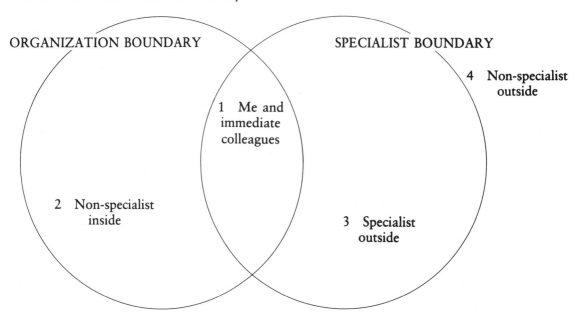

and with what effects for learning. Put the information on slips as shown in Figure 4.2. Their format should be adapted to fit the chosen piece of curriculum. Students will have let you know what is going on in their discussion with you. Indeed, the whole activity could be made the basis for further discussion. Ask them what they learn with you that they also learn in other ways (a suitable case for brainstorming). Decide with them how the slips should be set out to cover that ground. Ask them each to make out, and compare with each other, their analyses of what they are getting from where. That could be helpful to them. It could also be helpful to you.

FIGURE 4.2   Contribution to curriculum slips

	What happens?	What is intended?	What results?
US SPECIALISTS			
THOSE COLLEAGUES			
OUTSIDE SPECIALISTS			
OTHER OUTSIDERS			

The activity is designed to raise possibilities:

- for seeing how your work is, and is not, linked to what others are doing and for knowing what students are getting from what
- for talking with those other contributors, so that you know what they are doing and they know what you are doing
- for joint planning with partners, so that what you each do is mutually complementary, which might mean changing what you do
- for identifying common ground and conflicts between their intentions and your own
- for considering what, if anything, needs to be done about that.

We are invited to produce a curriculum which is more relevant to the problems and decisions which people need to make in our society now. The trouble is that what one group regards as more relevant another will regard as downright subversive. Also, the more diversely help is recruited into the provision of that curriculum, the more likely it is that these conflicts will occur.

The conflicts between, say, 'blue', 'green' and 'red' intentions for curriculum may turn out to be bigger in the minds of providers than they are in the minds of students. That possibility is addressed in the following section, leaving aside, for the moment, any reference to colour-coded conflict.

INPUT

A NEEDS-BASED CURRICULUM

Examination of experience of people both in and out of paid employment yields a recurring list of credits that people seek and need from their life and work and of deficits they incur when things go badly. The list is useful to teachers because all parts of all exisiting curricula are capable of being applied to the pursuit of at least one kind of credit or the avoidance of at least one kind of deficit.

One immediate practical use of the list would be to ask what contribution you and others are making, or could make, to help young men and women pursue any of these needs.

PRAGMATIC NEEDS

Most people need goods and seek to avoid poverty. The basic needs for goods are for food, shelter and clothing, although most people in our society feel that they need more than these necessities. Money is the primary means by which goods are exchanged and so most people express this need in terms of a need for money. Employment has been the chief means by which people gain money. Students can be helped to learn how to translate skills and knowledge into money through paid employment and through other means; they can be taught to trade and to barter, to budget and to conserve, to share and to negotiate and they can be taught to spot opportunities for the provisions of other people's practical needs, on a giving, sharing, selling or bartering basis.

PLANNING NEEDS

Most people need security and seek to avoid shapelessness in the unfolding of their lives. In its basic form the need for security is the need to know what to expect, to be able to anticipate and prepare for what is to come and to prepare for, and insure against, the worst that can be expected. But most people would like to be able to count on more than that. Employment stamps predictable rhythm on people's lives, providing times to start and to stop, a basis for anticipation and hope. With or without paid employment, students can be helped to learn how to anticipate and plan, how to organize time (in the short and long term), how to deal with the unforeseen, how to use group resources to deal with what individual resources cannot meet and they can be helped to understand and respond to other people's needs for security.

ATTACHMENT NEEDS

Most people need attachments to others and seek to avoid loneliness. In its most specific sense it is a need for companionship with other people: to understand them and be understood by them, perhaps to work with them. In its most general sense it is the need for a feeling of attachment to a community (it can be a kind of tribalism). Employment has been one of the chief means by which such a sense of attachment can be gained; it has also been one of the chief means by which individual personal contact has been established. Students can be helped to learn how to establish and maintain contact with individuals and groups, to understand and be understood, to find the personal resources for membership, empathy and cooperation with others and they can be helped to comprehend and alleviate other people's separation, isolation and loneliness.

ESTEEM NEEDS

Most people need esteem, nobody wants to be 'a nobody'. People demand respect and want to feel needed, to be able to contribute: a basis for confidence. For some the need for esteem extends to a hunger for positive pride, applause, status or acclamation. Paid employment has been a source of esteem; frequently, it is invested with snobberies and inverted snobberies. Loss of paid employment is experienced as humiliation. Students can be helped to learn how to gain a sense of esteem; about how to identify what is worthwhile in self, how to gain the attention, acknowledgement and respect of others for one's own worthwhileness, how to present self to others successfully, how to deal with lack of respect in others; also, they can be helped to comprehend and acknowledge the needs of others for basic respect and for esteem.

STIMULATION NEEDS

Most people seek stimulation and seek to avoid boredom. The search for stimulation is the search for something to respond to; the engagement of the senses, skills, intelligence and sensibilities. In young men and women the nerve ends can tingle for the lack of anything that provokes a response. If experience is not offered that is bright, attractive, interesting, engaging or stimulating, then it will be contrived, not always in socially acceptable ways. Paid employment can offer stimulation; the lack of paid employment is reported frequently as boring. Students can be helped to learn how to engage self in the environment in a way which is stimulating, to discover and understand what it is in self that seeks such rewards, to sharpen and to take pleasure in the sharpening of those attributes, to use what is found and developed in self in a variety of ways (both in and out of employment settings) and they can be helped to enrich experience for self and others.

INFLUENCE NEEDS

Most people seek influence and seek to avoid entrapment. Everybody wants to feel that her or his existence makes a difference to the way things get done, nobody wants to be pushed and pulled like a cork in the currents and vortices of impulses and events. That means being able to handle oneself; it also means being able to handle other people. Paid employment provides opportunities for such handling; it is a way of putting one's own mark on life. Lack of paid employment is reported frequently as a sense of uselessness and powerlessness. Students can be helped to learn how to use each her or his own personal influence in the world, to assert themselves, to resist manipulation by others, to make their own decisions and accept responsibility for themselves, to be 'political', to accept responsibility for what happens as a consequence of their actions; and they can be helped to respect the rights of other people to influence over their lives and environments.

- The list is written to relate to the rewards and deficits of having and not having work. However, the deficits described are also incurred by many people in jobs and others (the aged, infirm and house-bound spouse) on the margins of society.
- All the ideology of education for enterprise and employable capability can be found in the list. Some won't approve unless it's competitive in that way.
- But, although some can't approve unless it's competitive, others can't if it is; they may look for, and can find, the stuff of a humane and ecological education.
- While others, distrustful of the possibility of exploitation, will find in the list the stuff of education for assertive self-expression.
- The list is not analysed for ideological colour, but for types of motivation. It is about what people want, not about what other people want for them. It explains work not in terms of other people's 'work ethic', but in terms of individual need.

Sources: the analysis, adapted from Maslow (1954), the original form of which has been used in career-development theory by Roe (1956), is based on collations of more recent evidence, particularly on the career development of 14–19-year-olds (Law and Ward, 1981) and the impact of unemployment on young men and women (Law, 1983).

EXAMPLES

IS IT WORKING?

Short accounts of young men and women seeking out and implementing working lives are given in the following pages. None of the work described is conventional paid employment. It is not that this book is designed to ignore the needs of people who get jobs; it is that the experiences of people who won't, can't or, anyway, don't, get jobs are less-well documented and are no less illustrative of the importance of motivation for work. Actually, human needs are not much changed by the fact that there are, or are not, available jobs.

The accounts were designed originally for use with students (Law and Storey, 1986), but they are also used in curriculum- and staff-development work with teachers and others. They are examples of the sort of case material that can be used to monitor the relevance-to-need of curriculum development, asking to what extent any programme of work is responding to the needs of such young men and women, as well as to the needs of youngsters who will get jobs. Discussion of students' needs can lead to the expression of potential conflicts concerning the kind of problems we want our people to be able to solve and the kinds of decision we want them to be able to make. That is a necessary precursor to the finding of common ground.

Eileen's a writer

Eileen writes poems, stories and articles that she knows she can sell as leaflets on the streets of the city. Much of what she writes is about being on the dole, like her. Some of it is based on talking to people in her home town. She borrows a typewriter and copier from the youth centre, makes enough copies to sell, hitches a ride into the city and earns enough to finance the cost of her next production.

Jane's a dealer

Jane buys out of jumble sales she sees advertised in the local papers and sells into town-centre bric-a-brac shops. She makes around fifty pounds a week by knowing what to buy in the sale and how much to ask for it in the shop. It uses up Friday evenings and the weekends. She has a job during the rest of the week.

Jonathan's a furniture restorer

Jonathan did up a brass and iron Victorian bed his dad had bought. It was mainly for something to do, during the slow time on the farm, where he lives and works. Pleased and proud about the result, he looked around junk shops for another and borrowed the money to buy it. Profit from the first sale financed two more. Advertising in the local paper means he can sell as many as he can locate and work on. A local branch of a national chain of fabric stores has borrowed one for a window display, giving Jonathan free and valuable advertising. He prices his items by studying brochures and magazines. He calculates that he makes about five pounds for every hour he spends searching and restoring. It could be a living, if he wanted to take on the storage, planning and accounting problems that expansion would bring.

Errol's a bike technician

Errol and his mates put a postcard in the neighbourhood shop window offering to fix bikes, lawnmowers, anything that can be handled with the tools and experience they have between them. They don't charge much, little more than pocket money, but they get enough 'business' to occupy them 2–4 days each week.

Sheila's a musician

Sheila plays the drums in a local rock group. They spend a lot of time practising. Sheila took a job doing early-morning deliveries so that she can have time to practice. They get occasional gigs: village halls, school and club events, that sort of thing. But the money barely covers their expenses.

Sam's a puppeteer

Sam makes puppets in the garden shed. He and his mates have set up a puppet theatre which they tour round the neighbourhood: sometimes from the back of their hand-drawn cart, sometimes in halls. They get coins from passers-by and the occasional fee, but by the time they have paid their costs it doesn't add much to their dole money.

Harbhinder's a campaigner

Harbhinder worked with fellow students on a survey about the building of a local bypass; it was part of their course in social studies. But they found out things that local newspapers were denying. So they sent their findings to local radio and now everybody in the district knows that there are strong arguments for not doing what the authorities are proposing. Harbhinder is campaigning for the rerouting of the road.

Jean's a showbiz big-shot

Jean noticed local kids trying to find good surfaces for break-dancing in town. So she found out how much it was to hire the dance hall for an afternoon, rented it with her savings, calculated how many 'customers' she could expect and so worked out the entrance fee. It was a risk, but it paid off; she got enough takers to make a profit. The dance-hall management like it: they sell more eats and drinks. They want her to put on more shows. She's left her job in a local factory; she likes this better and hopes it can make her enough to live on.

Darren's an importer

Darren was still at school when his teacher noticed his money-making talents and encouraged him to start a company. He was studying maths, accounts, commerce and law. He reckons they have all helped to get his business going well. Using his own money he started buying sweets from wholesalers and selling them at school. He finds he can make a modest profit and still undercut the school tuck shop. He has done well enough to bring three other people into the business. He became the sole distributor of an Italian fizzy sweet by persuading the managing director of the British importing company that he was the best man able to market and sell it. Still a student at school, he makes more than twenty pounds a week.

Les is a motorbike-spares dealer

Les, Chas and Mike are out of a job, but they know about motorbikes. They know which have the most expensive spare parts and which parts people need most to be able to buy. They can also dismantle a bike and recondition its components. They raise enough money to buy crashed bikes of the right type: expensive spare parts in great demand. They find what they want in specialist magazines and they use the same magazines to advertise a mail-order spare-parts service. They've learned how to spot the right machines, how to price the items and how to avoid being ripped-off by crooks. They can make about twenty pounds a week each. If they want to make more they are going to have to borrow money.

Jack's a pigeon breeder

Jack breeds pigeons for sale. He has been doing so since he was in the third year at school. He learned it from his dad. Now, without a job, he finds he can get enough business to make extra pocket money on top of his dole cheque. He has made himself a county-wide reputation.

Caroline's a fund raiser

Caroline is the treasurer of her local Conservative Party. When she took over her job she found that most of the members were tired of holding the usual jumble sales. She decided to try out new ways of raising money. After talking it over with a few others she has organized a 'work exchange'. Party members do small jobs for each other: helping with things like decorating, fixing washing machines, gardening, baby-sitting and so on. The person who has the job done pays one pound an hour to party funds. Caroline keeps a register of the jobs which members are willing to do and she acts as the contact point for people who have work they would like done. The exchange makes a little more money than the jumble sales used to and party members seem to know each other better now.

Alex is a broadcaster

Alex uses his tape-recorder to make programmes on local issues in his city. He's made programmes about racism, the development of dockland areas, unemployment, anything that concerns local people. Practice has made him good at linking the voices of local people with music from local bands. He has been told that his material is good enough to broadcast, but the quality of the recording is not up to standard. He is trying to raise the money from a trust, so that he can get a better tape-recorder.

Joyce and Christopher are archaeologists

Joyce and Christopher have a huge collection of historic farm machinery, which they open to school parties during the summer term, and to the general public one weekend a month. It started while they were still at primary school. They found a fifteenth-century plough buried in their family's 3-acre garden. They've been collecting ever since. When they were in their last year at school they held an open-day. Since then farmers throughout the county have given them examples of machinery, from scythes to tractors, which they thought worth preserving. Joyce and Christopher have received sponsorship for the museum from the county council and a national chemicals company. They put a lot of time and energy into the museum, but they both also work on their father's farm. Any money raised from the museum is donated to charity.

Tracy's a photographer

Tracy's camera is a way of communicating what she sees and feels about what is happening in her patch. She photographs people at their work, children at play, anything and everything that's going on. She believes it's important to have records of people's lives. She wants to show it the way she sees it. While she's waiting for her government training course to start, she goes to evening classes in photography. It gives her the skills and, importantly, the darkroom facilities she needs. She shows her pictures only to people she trusts. She enjoys listening to their comments. Some say she's good! But she can't persuade herself to try to sell her pictures. She doesn't feel she's good enough. But she is no less serious about it because it doesn't make her any money.

Source: Law and Storey, 1986.

EXPLORATION

SECOND THOUGHTS ON PRE-VOCATIONAL EDUCATION

CURRICULUM, ASSESSMENT, ORGANIZATION AND PEDAGOGY

Pre-vocational education, like so many other concepts of education, defies exact definition. It absorbs, extends and, in some cases perhaps, supplants a great deal of earlier thought and practice. It has, for example, taken on board ideas of team-teaching, cross-curricular work, careers education, guidance and counselling, participative methods, experiential learning, work experience, recording achievement, life and social skills, education-for-industry, student-centred reviewing, negotiating curriculum, modular timetabling and education-for-capability. There is little new essentially in even its most thoroughgoing proposals.

But it has become a broader and, potentially, more powerful way of speaking about education than its predecessors. It is broader because it fuses a great deal of earlier thought into a coherent whole. It is, potentially, more powerful because it cannot be hived-off into a marginal position. It is proposed, not as a supplement to curriculum, nor as a tuning-up of curriculum, but as a root-and-branch reapplication, not only of curriculum, but also of assessment, organization and pedagogy.

ASSESSMENT

Assessment raises issues for how we know what is being gained. It is one of the means teachers use to know whether students have learned anything. It is also one of the means by which teachers are held to account; good examination results are quantifiable evidence of achievement, by both students and teachers. It is not surprising to find therefore that teachers teach what they know is going to be assessed. Profiling is a design feature of all well-developed proposals for pre-vocational education, in part, because it is well understood, not least by teachers themselves, that curriculum is shackled by assessment. If we want to change curriculum we must also change assessment. Experiments in profiling now offer a range of techniques for setting down what students have done and what they can do. Bolder experiments take students into the portrayal, not only of what they can do, but also into reflection on what they want: into motivational considerations (Law, 1984).

ORGANIZATION

Organization raises issues for who is to be involved. Pre-vocational proposals intend the re-organization of schooling in at least two respects. It is expected that each curriculum objective will be pursued by coordinated teams of teachers. It breaks the assembly-line classification of curriculum in which, subject-by-subject, students are wheeled around for the piecemeal accumulation of parts. The modularization of timetable, team-teaching techniques and cross-curricular work require that what each discipline contributes is made part of a whole. This is a serious intrusion into the way in which schooling is organized traditionally.

But pre-vocational education has another, more radical, answer to the question of who is to be involved. It is a design feature of thoroughgoing proposals that students are put into direct and personal contact with sources of learning in the community, usually in industrial and commercial work experience (Watts, 1983). The impact is, and, in part, is intended to be, that these offers of the pre-vocational franchise will change curriculum content. It is curriculum reform achieved by requiring a wider group to consider what sort of problems we want our people to be able to solve and what decisions we want them to be able to make. Schooling will develop different answers to those questions only if it is coaxed into relaxing its departmental classification and institutional framing of boundaries (Bernstein, 1971).

PEDAGOGY

Pedagogy raises issues for how we handle ourselves with students. Pre-vocational proposals support specific pedagogic trends. Promotional and support material is peppered with references to participative and experiential methods, broadening emphasis from the authority of teachers' knowledge, to include their skills as stimulators of self-propelled learning. Teachers are invited to conceive their roles, not so much as expert transmitters of curriculum content, but as managers of learning processes and resources. Terms like counselling, student-centred reviewing and curriculum negotiation express the intention that teachers understand the use that students do, and are able to, make of learning opportunities. They require a conception of teaching which invites students into partnership with teachers. Curriculum that pursues autonomous capability requires processes which exercise autonomous capability (Bates, 1983).

Teachers have, of course, been doing all of this for some time; often, as in the early use of work experience, with little support from policy makers and, usually, on a shoe-string. There are two new features in the situation: (1) central policy, funding and commercial interests now support the action and (2) curriculum is being handled in its mutual dependence with assessment, organization and pedagogy. With all four engines well fuelled, running hot and pointed in the same direction there is, so to speak, some chance of reaching escape velocity.

CAPABILITY, MOTIVATION, AWARENESS AND ATTACHMENT

Education-for-capability is counterpoised against mere academic learning : head learning, crammed by conventional curriculum, for examination success, and indicative of little but the ability to be successful in examinations. The problems we want our people to be able to solve, and the decisions we want them to be able to make, are, it is argued, problems and decisions for life and work in our society. Learning how to absorb and reproduce information is not enough. Students must be helped to learn problem-solving and decision-making skills.

Fundamentalists have argued that liberal and general education should have no part in post-16 pre-vocational courses. If that means that students are not to be helped except as required for functional performance, then it is subeducational in intent. It is easy, too easy, to dismiss academic learning as irrelevant; the term has more noble connotations than 'examination-bound'. It also connotes a capacity for abstract and formal thought, an ability to organize perceptions into concepts and to check, criticize and reform them. In this intellectual ability lies the human capacity to articulate the possible as well as the actual, the desired as well as the required and the precariousness of conventional configurations of reality: all the human potential for humour, art, science and other subversions of the status quo. A merely functional education could, conceivably, prevent students from developing further the intellectual basis for effective dissent. It would assign education-for-capability roughly the same significance as training for performing seals. No educational argument for education-for-capability implies that the skills to be developed are to be merely functional: articulated to socially defined requirements. The concept is important, not for its social usefulness, but for its insistence that the raising of awareness, development of concepts and identification of attitudes are active and operational skills and cannot be acquired through (indeed, will be hindered by) the passive absorption of other people's right answers, correct concepts and wholesome attitudes.

However, the concept of education-for-capability is troublesome in other ways. It permits the inference that lack of capability is part of the cause of economic decline. Actually, no educationist supporting education-for-capability has, in so many words, ever said that. It is imperative to dissociate it from simplistic, and politically convenient, arguments for off-loading blame for poor industrial and commercial performance to young men and women, and teachers.

But, whatever the politics, the education-for-capability movement does imply that, when young people do not do what is required of them, it is because they can't. The problem identified by education for capability is lack of capability. Therefore part of the conceptualization of pre-vocational education has been the identification of skills required by different 'families' of jobs; skills which, once acquired, can be transferred flexibly from job to job, as the labour economy changes, giving the student ownership of the skills for application and reapplication in a variety of future settings.

The explanation for non-performance could be, not just that they can't, but that they won't. Skills come attached to people; people also have feelings of attachment and aversion concerning what they do. The problem may be less about capability, more about motivation, less about 'can do' more about 'will do'. Teachers who have first-hand experience of the non-academic ability of youngsters to grease and fix what they want, when they want it, might agree.

The importance of motivation in career development has been well understood by educationists and industrialists for a long time (Daws, 1968). Re-analyses of more recent evidence suggest that explanations of career development which leave motivation out of account leave out too much (Law and Ward, 1981). Capable use of hand tools with commitment and enthusiasm for making and mending, and joy in the tactile experience of shaping materials to one's will, is different from the use of hand tools as a product of mere manual dexterity and coordination. No teacher and no employer is uninterested in the difference.

Studies also suggest that young adults are as likely as not to pay attention to their attachments to, and aversions for, people in the warp and weft of their social lives (Law, 1981). Nobody should assume that young Norman Clegg is going to uproot from all that attaches him to Holmfirth, just because he happens to have skills which are saleable in Hoddesdon.

The terms motivation and attachment are jargon for what, in another literature, might be called hopes, aspirations, enthusiasms, dreams, fears, yearnings, even loves. The concept of education-for-capability does not, necessarily, express them. It is true that pre-vocational education has other features which require that students are offered opportunities to reflect on the significance to them of what is being offered in schooling: counselling, student-centred reviewing and negotiated curriculum are examples. But curriculum has more to offer the education of motivation and attachment than that. Curriculum is the richest source of cultural material to be found anywhere in our society.

There is no subject on any curriculum which is incapable of being used to help students identify, order, conceptualize, articulate and pursue their needs and cultivate their attachments. If academic curriculum can be unshackled from the mere pursuit of examination credits it has much more to offer pre-vocational education than any formula for education-for-capability has yet uncovered.

WHAT COUNTS AS VOCATION IN PRE-VOCATIONAL EDUCATION?

There is a perennial problem about terms in this field. Before the term pre-vocational became common coinage the problem was for careers. A symptom was that, during the 1960s and 1970s, the term was seldom used singly. We have a National Association of Careers and Guidance Teachers, a Counselling and Careers Development Unit and a National Institute for Careers Education and Counselling. The problem was that the term 'careers' sets boundaries around what experience requires to be liberated. People do not, it was argued, handle careers in isolation from all the other problems and decisions they have to forge from the capabilities, motivations and attachments in their lives. Career development is but one, rather arbitrarily defined, occasion for addressing whom I am becoming (Rogers, 1965).

The nature of the problem can be illustrated from what was, for a time, a conventional fourfold analysis of the aims of careers education (Law and Watts, 1977). (1) Opportunity awareness helps students to know what is in the structure of opportunities available in society: its demands, access points, the alternatives; it is meant to bring students to the point where they can answer for themselves the question 'where am I?'. (2) Self-awareness helps students to know and respect themselves: what they can do, what they are like and what they want; it is meant to bring students to the point where they can answer the question 'who am I?'. (3) Decision learning helps students grasp and use the skills, styles, risks and responsibilities of decision making; it is meant to bring students to the point where they can answer the question 'what will I do?'. (4) Transition learning helps students gain and sharpen their skills and strategies for getting from one stage in their lives to the next; it is meant to bring students to the point where they can answer the question 'how will I cope?'.

The problem is that the answers to each of these questions are intertwined with answers to questions about sex, social-class and ethnic identity and each can be applied as validly to domestic, social, leisure, parental and political roles. Careers counselling has been found not to process on the basis of reflecting only about careers, it opens up to much more. Careers lessons have been expanded in content to the point where people begin to wonder what the differences are between their objectives and the objectives of education-as-a-whole.

The arbitrariness of the term careers education is magnified by rising rates of youth unemployment. The term pre-vocational education is not exempt from all these charges of arbitrariness. To offer pre-vocational education as a way of improving the chances of getting a job could prove to be a cruel deception. No doubt some employers, meeting some students who have achieved some gains, will be inclined to offer vacancies that otherwise would not have been offered. That adds to the pool of jobs available to young workers, but at a level out of all arithmetic balance with the magnitude of the problem and, in some cases, at the expense of older workers. Beyond that, the best that job-orientated pre-vocational education can achieve in a relatively contracting labour economy is a change in the pecking order for available jobs. We will not get a quart into a pint pot by improving the quality of the beer.

The accounts of young people's experience given previously in this chapter raise issues for what counts as vocation in pre-vocational education. The identities and roles they are developing have breadth and variety, adding further to the concept of career connotations of cultural, artistic, media, political as well as self-employed enterprise. To articulate either career or pre-vocation exclusively to the pursuit of paid employment would be unacceptably arbitrary. To do so in the context of continuing high rates of youth unemployment would be like training performing seals in an ever-decreasing circus.

ACTION
PRE-VOCATIONAL AUDIT

This action extends the activity suggested at the beginning of the chapter further. Like the activity, it can be undertaken by a single teacher re-examining her or his work with students. But it can also be used as basis for a departmental or institutional pre-vocational curriculum audit. It leads to a diagnosis of what activities use what resources to pursue what pre-vocational intentions and provides a basis for further action (Figure 4.3).

A framework is described here, that can be adapted to make as finely tuned an analysis as you want. More thoroughgoing versions can, for example, make separate analyses for each year-cohort of students. It first requires that intentions are organized into headings. The needs-based analysis of curriculum objectives and the fourfold analysis of careers

FIGURE 4.3   Framework for audit

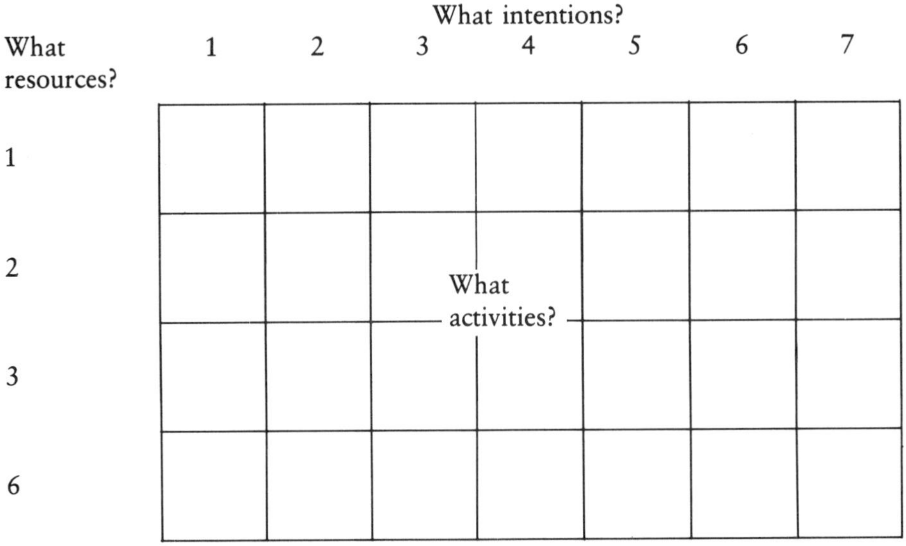

education (both set out previously in this chapter) are only two of many possible means of ordering pre-vocational intentions. Decide how to analyse the intentions in the programme, without falling into the trap of merely repeating the headings in the syllabus(es).

Resources are analysed in the same way as for the activity in Chapter 1.

(1) Inside specialist action: what is done by people who have a formal and designated responsibility for the pursuit of pre-vocational intentions?
(2) Inside general action: what is done informally or by people who work in departments which have no designated responsibility for the pursuit of pre-vocational

FIGURE 4.4   Detailed framework

Resources	Descriptions of action	Pre-vocational intentions						
		1	2	3	4	5	6	7
1 INSIDE	a							
SPECIALIST	b							
	c							
2 INSIDE	a							
GENERAL	b							
	c							
3 OUTSIDE	a							
SPECIALIST	b							
	c							
4 OUTSIDE	a							
GENERAL	b							
	c							

intentions? (this is the use of the first and second franchises, as described in Chapter 3).

(3) Outside specialist action: how are contributions made by people based outside the organization and with a formal responsibility in pre-vocational work?

(4) Outside general action: how are contributions made by people from everyday adult working life in the community? (this is the third franchise, as described in Chapter 3).

It has been found useful to set out the information as shown in Figure 4.4.

The analysis makes cells in which information about impact can be coded. That means knowing how much of what is being offered to which students with what effect. Tongue-in-cheek codes might include A (students gain what is intended), through C (some do, some don't), to E (they haven't the faintest idea what they are supposed to be getting from it) and perhaps even to X (they don't use it for our purposes, they use it for their own!). Try out and refine a coding system for which you can gain the information and which gives you a picture of what is happening now.

Where, for example, a careers officer comes in to interview some third-year students on the way in which they weigh up the pros and cons concerning course options, then the analysis would describe that activity in row 3, entered (say) under a column headed decision learning to show intention and coded to show impact. It might look like the entry shown in Figure 4.5.

The audit can be useful on planning which:

● requires the articulation of intentions, the listing of resources, the description of activities and the assessment of impact, forcing a review (in the case of team use, a discussion) of what curriculum is for and where the hot spots for future resolution and decision making lie

● identifies the range of intentions being pursued by the programme, raising questions about how much effort is being assigned to what intentions and what sort of balance is being achieved in that respect

● requires a review of impact, raising questions about the relation between intentions and the use students can and do make of them, in particular, perhaps, raising questions about the whether their unintended use of curriculum might not be more relevant to their needs

FIGURE 4.5 Example of entry

Resources	Descriptions of action	Pre-vocational intentions			
		1 Decision learning	2	3	4
3 OUTSIDE SPECIALIST	a CO ind'l intvws on options	20% of Yr3: impact not known			

- identifies what use is made of a range of schooling and community-linked resources, raising questions about what use is made of the range, what is under-resourced, whether there is, and should be, duplication and what untapped resources might be brought into coordinated partnership with the programme
- does so systematically, suggesting where next action might best lie; intentions might be augmented and rebalanced; impact might be monitored to inform changes; new resources might be identified and canvassed.

Source: Law and Watts, 1977.

CHAPTER 5

CLOUT AND WISDOM

In this chapter the following are examined critically:

- how you have sought to influence events
- what other means of influence there may be
- how people have used different styles of influence in community-linked activity
- how action can get mooted, explored and agreed among a range of partners.

According to Dr. Marlon Corleone of the Sicilian Institute, change is brought about by making offers that cannot be refused. It is argued that government action, to encourage new curriculum development by offering substantial grants to schooling which conforms to policy, is the best confirmation yet of the validity of the Corleone theory of educational change. Yet Professor Thomas Jerry of Peoria University holds out some prospect for effective muscular intervention by minions, although confirmation of the theory is still awaited in education settings.

There are those who, against recent evidence, insist that H. B. Finn's early theoretical work is still viable. Dr. Finn, at Missouri's Huck Academy, argues that there is little evidence that people at the top have enough wisdom, usefully, to control the course of events and that we must train and encourage grass-roots people to use their heads, rather than their muscle, to bring about needed changes.

Questions about just how much wisdom or clout there is at the top and bottom of the education system must, for the time being, remain open. This chapter opens with an invitation to you to consider the evidence of your own experience.

ACTIVITY

SPRINGS FOR ACTION

This activity is based on a chart (see Figure 5.1) on which you can enter three accounts of your own attempts to bring about change, get things done in a different way or

FIGURE 5.1   Springs for action: accounts of situations

Situations	Account
a	When I [. . .]
b	When I [. . .]
c	When I [. . .]

influence people. They may be successful or unsuccessful, professional, domestic or whatever, but it will be better if they are recent. You may have been the sole promoter or part of a team; concentrate on your own activity. Call the situations a, b and c.

The chart invites you to analyse your actions, according to whether you used positional, bargaining, personal, consultative or expert influence and how you managed that influence.

- Positional influence relies on an agreement that your role in the organization (school, college, family, church or wherever) has a right to influence. Bosses get things done because they are in a position to do so. Children may obey parents, in part anyway, from respect for their position. Positional influence is an acknowledgement that the way you say it will be is the way it will be. Other people may be in no position to deny that.

- Bargaining influence relies on being able to offer or withhold what others want. Or it relies on being able to impose or withdraw what is not wanted. It 'deals', making your action contingent on theirs. It may say 'I will help in these ways if you will do that'. It invites them to calculate benefits and resources against expenditure of effort. It is not the exclusive prerogative of bosses. Some bargaining is done by people who are not members of the organization.

- Personal influence wins action on the basis of attachment to you as a person; they do it because it is you who ask them. The attachment is positive: liking or admiration for you. Just being a friend can be enough to win a response. If the attachment is accompanied by excitement and commitment about being associated with you, then the response can be greater. Personal influence requires personal visibility. It can be found at all levels in any hierarchy.

- Consultative influence entails understanding their situation and seeking a basis for action which uses that understanding. That means listening to what they have to say, comprehending it, reflecting it in what you say and arriving at a proposal for action which is, at the end, as much their suggestion as it is yours. Not only do you not have to be a boss to exercise such influence, you do not need to have membership in the organization. But it requires contact which permits an exchange of views between you and them.

- Expert influence relies on your ability to generate knowledge which is a useful basis for action. It requires that you can do that, that the knowledge is useful and that they will pay attention to it. It entails enquiry, evidence, ideas and argument. You do not have to be a member of the organization to exert such influence. Neither does it require that you are as personally visible or accessible to them as personal and consultative influences do. It is influence, however, which requires their acknowledgement of your authority.

● All forms of influence can be managed differently. Some influence is managed cautiously: prepared to wait; carefully monitoring responses to first steps before

FIGURE 5.2   Profile of influence

	My part in situation a	My part in situation b	My part in situation c	Total Rank %
1 I used my position for creating a sense of what is *expected* in action				T
				R
				%
2 I made a deal, offering something in *exchange* for action				T
				R
				%
3 I used my personality, generating *enthusiasm and commitment* for action				T
				R
				%
4 I used my grasp of other people's concerns, *talking them through their case* for action				T
				R
				%
5 I used my expertise, *arguing* the case for action				T
				R
				%
6 I was bold, *pressing* for radical new action				T
				R
				%

Dominant methods in each situation

embarking on subsequent steps; taking account of reactions, and adjusting on that basis, mindful of unanticipated consequences. Some is managed boldly: in a hurry, assuming the rightness of the proposal; pressing for implementation, mindful of the ease with which time can be wasted by too much agonizing over problems.

Use the chart shown in Figure 5.2 to describe your actions in the three situations. Put down in each box what you did to exert influence in that particular respect, in that situation. You could, of course, be kidding yourself about this, making yourself look the way you want to see yourself. Feedback might be useful. One way of getting feedback would be to make a profile of your styles and show it to somebody who knows you well. No such profile could be useful for more than discussion purposes.

To make a profile you need to score each of the entries in the six boxes in each column, by giving the dominant style in each action the highest score and assigning the others appropriately lower scores. It doesn't matter what range of score you choose (1–3, 1–6, 1–10 are all possibilities). Choose the range and spread your scores on it as you decide. Put them in the small boxes.

FIGURE 5.3 Styles of information

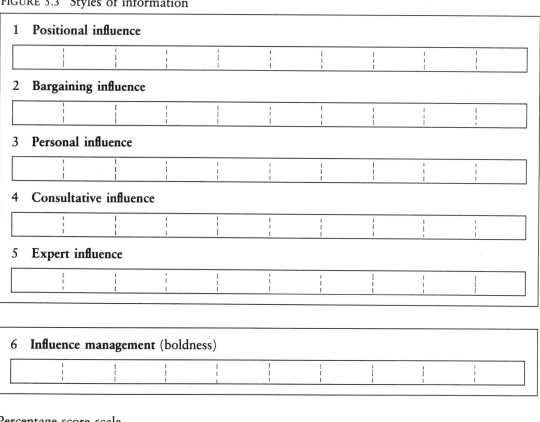

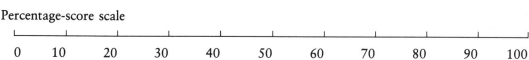

Percentage-score scale

Total your scores for each style on the right and rank order the styles on this basis. But to make a comparable profile you need to calculate percentages; that is the percentage of the total-of-all-scores in all actions.

$$\frac{\text{Total for this style}}{\text{Total for all styles}} \times 100 = \text{percentage for this style}$$

A profile form, that you could use to see if others agree how you describe yourself, is shown in Figure 5.3. There are no right answers to these questions. Plots on the right of the profile are not necessarily better than plots on the left. It is not a bad idea, none the less, to see how far people agree with your own characterization of yourself and to see if there are any habitual ways you have of going about influencing events. Shade each row to the level which represents your diagnosis of your own usual ways of seeking to influence events.

You might find it useful to:

● mark on each scale the average score and range of scores for any group of colleagues with which you are working
● show your profile to somebody who knows you well and ask whether what it shows surprises him or her or not
● reflect on the respects in which your style of seeking to influence events has been effective or otherwise in any of the situations in which you have used them.

An analysis of some of the features of different sorts of influence appears in Figure 5.4. It is organized on two analyses: (1) influence based on *CLOUT* (leverage, power) versus influence based on *WISDOM* (knowledge, understanding) and (2) *BOLD* (radical, intervening) influence versus *CAUTIOUS* (low profile, careful) influence.

INPUT

REPERTOIRES FOR INFLUENCE

Whether exercised to change or to hinder change, whether exercised formally or informally, there is more than one source of influence open to most people in most organizations. You may find your usual ways of seeking to influence the course of events in the analysis following (Figure 5.4); also you may find suggestions concerning how your habitual ways of seeking to influence events may be extended.
You may furthermore be able to identify helpfully how other people have sought to influence events in which you have an interest.

EXAMPLES

AGENTS OF CHANGE?

On the following pages are examples of activity set out to illustrate different influencing styles. They are analysed, with other examples cited in this book, in a chart shown in

FIGURE 5.4   Planning for influence

1 Positional influence		
Giving feedback and approval	Establishing climate and expectations	Making requirements and demands
(normative)		(coercive)
2 Bargaining influence		
Offering contacts, things, status	Negotiating action for something in return	Making conditional 'high stake' offers
(remunerative)		('Godfather')
3 Personal influence		
Befriending and supporting	Suggesting and modelling	Inspiring and cajoling
(social interaction)		(charismatic)
4 Consultative influence		
Clarifying and reflecting	Restating and analysing	Interpreting and confronting
(problem solving)		
5 Expert influence		
Establishing enquiry and thought	Offering information and ideas	Disseminating and persuading
(research, development and diffusion)		

Left axis (vertical): ANALYSED FOR [...] [...] MORE WISDOM ... [...] MORE CLOUT

ANALYSED AS [...]
[...] MORE CAUTIOUS   [...] BOLDER
←——————————————————————→

(The words in parentheses are terms used in various attempts to characterize influence.)

TABLE 5.1   Agents of change: examples of positions and styles

Styles	Positions		
	Boss	Colleague	Outsider
Position	A2, A3, A4, A5, A6, B2, C1, F2	A6, A7, C2, D3	A6, D1
Bargaining	A2, A5, A6, B2, C1, D2	A4, A5, A7, C3, D3	D1, F3
Personal	B2	A1, C3, F1	B1, D1, F3
Consultative	A2, C1, D2	A1, A3, A4, A5, A6, A7, C2, C3, D3, F1, F2	A4, A5, A6, B1, D1, F3
Expert	A2, C1, D2	A2, D3, F2	A3, A4, A5, A6, B1, D1, F3
Management	A2, B2, D2	C3, D3, F1, F2	B1, D1, F2, F3

Table 5.1 where attention has been paid to the styles mentioned previously in this chapter: position, bargaining, personal, consultative, expert influence and influence management.

However, the chart pays attention to another feature: that is to the positions which the promoters have in the organizations in which the innovations are taking place. Where the promoters include senior members of the organizations, as at least one is in the curriculum survey at Furtherwick Park School (**D2**), the entries are headed 'boss'. Where the promoters are, largely, members of the organizations, but not in particularly senior positions, as in the Community Newspaper Project (**D3**), the entries are listed as 'colleagues'. Where the promoters are not members of the organizations, but are coming in to promote change, as they are in Clydebank EC Project (**D1**), the entries are listed as 'outsider'.

The multiple entries of projects in the rows as well as the columns of the chart reflects the fact that most action is promoted by more than one person. The codes refer to accounts to be found in other chapters (A in Chapter 1; B in Chapter 2; C in Chapter 3; F in Chapter 7). The accounts will prove useful to thought, discussion and planning on what styles are appropriate, in what sorts of situation and by promoters in different relations with the organization.

Agents of change: examples of positions and styles
_____

D1   Clydebank EC Project
_____

The concern of this European Community-funded 4-year project is to improve preparation for adult and working life in neighbourhood schools and to improve industry's understanding of schools and of young people's school experience. The setting is housing estates containing 'pockets of deprivation which are among the worst 1 per cent in the Strathclyde region'. The intention is to set up curriculum development, work experience, pre-employment courses, the use of community amenities and a range of assessment and profiling procedures and formats. A project team of three full-time staff intends to catalyse such cross-curricular development for small cohorts of students taken from 'lower achieving' groups in four (later two) schools. For implementation the project is dependent on 60 teachers in local schools and colleges. Funding for the release of these teachers is equivalent to seven full-time staff appointments. The project is evaluated externally.

Positional influence

The project officers form what the evaluators characterize as 'an umbrella' organization, identifying — with review by committees — the steps to be taken. Headteachers become the project's first producers; they produce proposals for a new curriculum framework which is circulated to participating schools. Yet the team finds it can coerce nothing; the approach is later characterized by a member of the team as 'diplomacy'; it is characterized by the evaluators as 'bureaucratic', by an adviser as 'a paper chase'.

Bargaining influence

More than 80 per cent of the budget is spent on staffing. Part of this money is available for teacher release, but — according to the evaluators — it proves insufficient to pay for intensive developmental task-group work over any length of time.

Personal influence

A variety of subprojects emerges, as task groups and staffed by school and college personnel, working, for example, on a communications course required by the curriculum framework. They are reported as 'grass-roots' developments, relying on the experience of the participants more than on centrally generated ideas. An adviser records regret that there is too little face-to-face contact between the 'umbrella' staff and 'chalkface' teachers. The project team are said by the evaluators not to 'model' with teachers the sorts of participative methods the team favours with students, i.e. involving people in the search for solutions.

Consultative influence

The early curriculum framework is developed by heads, independently of teachers — who, it is argued 'cannot be spared to participate in working parties preparing syllabuses'. Initial reactions of LEA advisers are that it is a mistake not to involve teachers in discussion at this stage. Evaluators are perceived as having discredited themselves by being too critical. Eventually, a newly appointed adviser for English — not part of the funded-project staff — responds to a request from a subproject for a communications course. He produces a discussion document, leading to a series of meetings in which he invites the subproject team to use their experience as professionals to design the course.

Expert influence

Teachers are reported to seek directives from 'experts'. Project managers gather ideas from projects elsewhere in the country and disseminate ideas of 'good practice'. A 2-day conference is held in which 'experts in a number of fields' participate. Where internal ideas are developed by the 'umbrella' they do not appear to the evaluators to have become familiar to 'grass-roots' workers or are regarded by them as too sketchy.

Influence management

The project is intended to be a radical cross-curricular development project. But it is also designed to use its own experience as a basis for action — by stages. The project proposal is reported to have been taken as the project's remit. This gives urgency to some early actions. But the resulting pressure is reported to have caused schools to 'turn inward'. In the end the project team characterize its influence as for 'adjustment' rather than 'big changes'.

The project produces courses in construction, home maintenance, trades union studies, communication and catering. It explores the validity and practicality of profiles and ways of integrating experiential learning with the curriculum. Its work has led to the commercial publication of a mini-cooperatives kit and a series of booklets on trade unions. It has developed the idea of 'transition tutor', integrating in one role aspects of teaching, pastoral care and vocational guidance. Also it has given a greater priority and motivation to the 'less able' than — it is claimed — is usual in Scottish schools, probably making those students more favourably disposed to further education and training opportunities. Evaluators claim that it is the subprojects which are more fruitful than the 'umbrella', although they initially lack overall coherence between schools. Their fruitfulness is explained in terms of the opportunity which advisers give to teachers to draw on their own authority and experience. Others argue that the 'umbrella' organization has been necessary to the development of subproject initiatives.

Sources: Strathclyde Department of Education, 1980a; Stronach and Weir, 1983; European Community Action Programme, 1984.

D2   Curriculum Survey at Furtherwick Park School

The concern is that more of this 11–16 comprehensive school's curriculum be brought to bear on the students' career development needs. The plan is promoted by the head of careers and a colleague with special responsibility for personal development. It is to establish a school-wide survey by questionnaire; of statements about what teachers see to be students' career-development needs; of estimates of the relevance, activity and success of current curriculum; of statements diagnosing the current situation as a basis for future development.

Positional influence

The survey is proposed as something that will be useful in the school; participation is requested by the head of careers. Careers education is already well established in the school.

Bargaining influence

The findings will be tabulated and returned to all members of staff. The results are also offered to all departmental meetings and to a meeting of the heads of department. The head of careers insists that the material will be useful to future decision making in the school.

Personal influence

There is no obvious evidence of personal pressure; except, perhaps, of that represented by the 'modelling' of thoroughness with which the 'careful, methodical scrutiny' is put together.

Consultative influence

Careers staff make themselves available as informal consultants to colleagues on the implications of the survey's findings concerning future curriculum development.

Expert influence

The head of careers — a self-confessed 'rationalist' — argues from a theoretical base, presents the survey as research with a significance both for this school and other schools; he bases the design of the survey on ideas taken from the literature of career development. The idea of the survey emerged during both teachers' participation in a course on prevocational curriculum- and organization-development.

Influence management

The whole project is modest initially, in comparison with what might have been envisioned for curriculum-development concerns. The questionnaire is designed to be manageable in 15 min. It is piloted in a similar school before being introduced to Furtherwick Park. A 2-week deadline for completion is extended to 3. Consultation is invited, not imposed or scheduled as a formal part of the process. Intentions are open-ended, left to initiatives to be taken by teachers.

The response rate to the questionnaire is 89 per cent. It is reported immediately to have enlivened interest in curriculum development. An account of the whole study is bound into a document available from the school. The survey contributes directly to the establishment of working parties to make proposals for action. The proposal finally adopted is for the establishment of a core-curriculum 'pre-vocational education' programme, occupying 30 per cent of students' time in the fourth and fifth years. The programme incorporates and reapplies curriculum material from science, physical education, religious education, 'health, politics and economics', money management, the law, computers, careers education, media studies, technology and homecraft. The programme is activity based and skill orientated. There is a community service and work-experience component. A records of achievement has been designed to portray students' participation in the programme.

Sources: Poulter and O'Connell, 1984; Furtherwick Park School, 1985.

D3   Community Newspaper Project

The concern is to use part of the existing core curriculum to put fourth-year students in touch with alternatives to paid employment. It is an area of high unemployment. The intention is to set up a joint English–social education project to produce a neighbourhood newspaper on 'alternative' work. It is being promoted by English and social-education teachers in the humanities faculty of the school.

Positional influence

An early approach is made by the English teacher to her head of department, who — in turn — approaches the headteacher. The head rejects the idea on the grounds that it could lead students into contact with 'doubtful' groups in the neighbourhood.

Bargaining influence

The head of English is, herself, worried about handing over too much departmental resource to such a project. The idea looks more acceptable when, later, social studies and English teachers agree to share the project. Back-to-back timetabling releases more than 3 hrs of continuous time each week. Some resources for the physical production of the paper are gained from interested parents; the project 'trades' for it with free advertising space in the paper.

Personal influence

Some teachers are affronted by the lumping together of CND and NF as 'doubtful groups' with which students should not be brought into contact. What could have become a bitter

— and probably a personal — argument is shelved in favour of a more consensual position.

Consultative influence

The English teacher has taken the idea from students who have learned about a wide range of 'alternative' working activity in the neighbourhood and suggested to her that they could make a newspaper about it in English. It is as much their idea as anybody's. When the English teacher realizes that social-education colleagues want to develop a project on 'wider concepts of work' she introduces the students' ideas to faculty meetings. As the project gets underway the teachers adopt the role of consultants to the various editorial and production teams that are set up by the students.

Expert influence

Argument for the idea is based on teachers' experience of cynicism among students concerning their own career prospects. The English and social-studies teachers decide to develop the idea further before trying to take it back to the head. They represent it as an argument for a programme with specified awareness-raising and skill-development objectives.

Influence management

The humanities team avoid confronting the 'doubtful groups' argument; they develop a united front by concentrating on the need of students to see that schooling can equip them for more than one working style, and that it is important to do this kind of work while they are still at school, and can be helped to reflect on what they are finding out. The project is put forward as an experiment; a pilot to test its value and use.

The project produces three of the five issues planned. The team begins to consider diversifying the programme so that other forms of media production can be developed in future years. The idea of a portfolio of each student's achievements is linked to the scheme. The team fears that it may prove difficult to get students to re-enter more conventional English and social-studies work in the fifth year of schooling.

Source: Law and Storey, 1986.

EXPLORATION

SECOND THOUGHTS ON TRYING TO INFLUENCE ANYTHING

TOP-DOWN?

The upward gaze of the grass-roots worker can betray a sense of entrapment by policy-initiated conditional offers from 'above'. But not all the influence is near 'the top'. Nor, to be fair, does the top, invariably, behave as though it believes it is. Much of what is fed down through the policy-making chains is not only first derived from grass roots, it invites continued development at grass roots.

There are mutual dependencies between all levels in stratified systems. The analysis given following, adapted from an ecology of child development (Bronfenbrenner, 1979), suggests that people are attached to complex systems at a variety of levels. It suggests that different people may elect to participate at different levels.

Some influence comes from a sense of responsibility for, and to, society (Bronfrenbrenner calls it the 'macrosystem'), with its pervasive beliefs, needs, ideologies and historical legacies. It is a sense that the audience to actions is that whole community. Some projects are addressed directly to that audience; it is a first action of the 'Elin' Community Group, reported in full later (F1), to ensure that it is reported in the press.

It can lead to policy concerns with education-for-capability, the failure of schooling or the future of work. Some discussion assumes that, unless overarching policies on such issues can be found among people in high places, then little can be done elsewhere. Part of the Clydebank EC Project's (D1) verdict on itself is that real change takes a long time because it requires national decisions rather than local initiatives. Its evaluators report the project as seeking policies for action which are thought to be high on national agendas.

Others modify that argument; some Education Work Councils (C1) are offered state legislation to mandate their activities in all communities. Wirtz (1975) argues against it; he wants a climate of support rather than direct bureaucratic intervention: 'The notion of a single national, largely publicly funded, approach to education-work issues is not a very realistic one.'

The survey at Furtherwick Park (D2) awaits no such directive from the top. The head of careers canvasses a general analysis of human needs (taken from the same source as that given in Chapter 4). The questionnaire to staff invites colleagues to say to what extent schooling responds to those needs. The intention is to develop and agree a generalized picture of people-in-society, in such a way as to know what is a good idea for schooling and what is not. Furtherwick Park School makes its own picture of the general nature of the situation.

Some people (because of the senior positions they occupy, or the budgets they command) are, or feel, obliged to take such macrosystematic views. But other people take such perspectives, and should.

Some influence comes from a sense of attachment to more-or-less recognizable constituencies within society (exosystems), such as industry and commerce, trade unionism, schooling, the churches, the unemployed, family life or alternative life styles. Most people would acknowledge some such sort of attachment, many to more than one. The sense of audience is to those specific constituencies.

It gives rise to talk of 'the needs of industry', 'the importance of family life', 'the rights of workers', or 'the plight of the unemployed'. The Community Newspaper Project (D2) is addressed to the condition of youngsters expressing bitter mirth concerning their own job prospects. People with such attachments can usually speak from a more defensible authority on such issues than they can for society-at-large. In community-linked schooling alliances and caucuses can form on such bases.

People see themselves as representing recognizable associations in which they have immediate membership ('mesosystems'), such as a school, a college department, a family, a factory, a section within a commercial firm, a commune, a cooperative or a trade-union branch. Almost everybody will acknowledge some such sort of attachment, most will acknowledge more than one.

It leads to talk of 'this is what we want', 'we do it another way' or 'we are resourced for that'. The authority of such voices is, in principle, harder to challenge from outside. But people representing mesosystems in community-linked activity are more likely (than people representing macrosystems or exosystems) to come from lower as well as higher hierarchical levels in the attachments they represent; although they have authority, they may not always get their voices heard.

However, action originates here, as well as elsewhere in the system. The evaluators of the Clydebank EC Project (**D1**) characterize the subprojects as less well-resourced than the umbrella organization, but with more specific concerns and plans. Early frustration at not getting sufficient detailed help from the 'umbrella' is reported to be met later by grass-roots workers producing for themselves what they feel they can use.

Some influence is people just speaking for themselves (Bronfrenbrenner's term is 'microsystems'), as distinct and individual voices for their own experience. That may be as a teacher speaking for her or himself (not all teachers), a parent, an employer or a student so-speaking. It evokes statements such as 'I can do that', 'that's not what happened to me' or 'my worry is for my children'. It is the natural basis on which parents, shop-floor workers and students will participate. It may be the basis on which heads of departments, consultants and managers prefer to participate, leaving those to speak for society or even the others, who think they can.

The individual participant is at the point of delivery to students. Her and his influence on what happens is always critical, but not always acknowledged or consulted. In the work of at least one of the subgroups in the Clydebank EC Project there is disagreement between heads of department about what sort of teaching and learning modules should be developed. The adviser uses his administrative position in the education authority (there is insufficient project finance for the task) to establish a series of meetings to get those disagreements voiced, later commenting 'committed, motivated, competent people are worth more than any amount of money, hot air, blarney and phoney claims'. Such voices are vulnerable to challenge from other levels of influence, which can easily make them sound weak. Yet it is the authority that most of us can be sure of; often it is the only authority we can be sure of.

The upward-gazing worker may assume too easily that there is greater aggregated power in higher levels of the system than at the grass roots. The Clydebank EC Project umbrella (characterized by the evaluators as a top-down, radical and well-resourced strategy) finally characterizes itself as 'settling for adjustments rather than big changes'. The evaluators regard the subprojects as being rather more fruitful than the umbrella. Yet, as the project leader portrays the situation finally, 'without the impetus of the project the subprojects would neither have existed nor produced ideas or materials'. The problem is for the release of authority at all levels in the ecology.

BOTTOM-UP?

Much of what emerges from the reports of change cited in Chapter 2 suggests the critical importance of grass-roots engagement. Users are, in particular, in a key position with regard to change. Their responses to it will transform it. That theme in Chapter 2 is summarized briefly here.

An organization is more ready for change where its boundaries are open, not only to central agencies exercising influence from a distance, but to the interactions with the day-to-day experience of its own people and neighbourhood. Exchanges between the departments sections and people in an organization, which foster the sharing of ideas and doubts about proposed action, collective-problem solving and the flexible allocation of the organization's resources, make readiness for change. Pressure or support from management guarantees nothing. Management may be as much a matter of sensing and using the winds and currents of organizational ambience as of redirecting action in a preplanned way.

Proposals for new action, whatever their origin, stand a better chance of survival where they make common ground with the preoccupations of audiences and users in a specific situation. There is a need for grass-root people to see the point of the proposal.

Different audiences and users respond to different styles of promotion in different ways. There is no ready-made script on how to promote an idea for change. The direct and personal negotiation with users of the idea and its methods can bring even imported ideas into the possession and ownership of users. Skilful promotion for change means anticipating the responses of audiences.

The sense of ownership is critical if people are not to be cast in the role of reluctant carriers of other people's baggage. Users, particularly in the early days, may experience anxiety concerning new suggestions. There is a need to acknowledge and deal with those anxieties if they are not to crystallize into erosive attitudes. People are reassured, and their attitudes change, at least as much on the basis of their own experience of use as on the basis of promotion by others. Users are as likely to learn from each other as they are from outside promotion. Hit-and-run promotion does not take account of the unanticipated and residual problems that users will experience with any proposed innovation. Part of the process of implementation is the sustained process of review and adaptation. The reactions of students are key influences in the sustainability of any initiative.

It is not surprising, then, to find the teachers on the Parkway Project (A2) characterizing their role with community contacts as one of 'finessing' their way into credibility and acceptance. Similarly, a school coordinator on the Industry Project in Cleveland (A4) characterizes his role as 'infiltrator'. The consultative skills of the teachers on the Transition to Working Life Project (A3) prove similarly subtle; characterized as maintaining a balance between respect for the authority of the working coach and yet seeking to offer substantive help, an offer of support without control.

TASKS AND SETTINGS

Any person or group who wants to exercise influence on the way things get done in schooling faces a subtle task. There is a range of settings in which such tasks may be pursued. In-service training is a major means by which influence is sought on schooling and it is salutary to ask to what extent what kinds of in-service training can be used as setting to pursue these tasks.

INFORMING

Informing provides audiences and users with material about what is entailed in what is proposed. The content of information includes answers to all the 'journalists's questions': what?, how?, when?, who? and, not least, why? There are skills to be used. The first proposals for curriculum made by the heads in the Clydebank EC Project (**D1**) are said, by the evaluators, to have 'landed on the desks', part of a 'paper chase', with too little face-to-face consultation with teachers, and suffering from sketchiness. Different audiences need different information. The industry project coordinator produces a flow of information sheets for trades unionists, employers and other groups, each worded to reflect the interests and preoccupations of the constituency to which they are addressed.

CANVASSING

Canvassing an idea for action means that the temperature of reaction is tested, by trawling for reactions in such a way as to ascertain what common ground there is between users' and audiences' preoccupations and what is being proposed. At Madeley Court School (**B2**) a series of staff-development sessions is used to canvass and discuss the ideas for community-linked education being promoted by the head and his immediate colleagues. The establishment of the mini-schools is not, at first, generally welcome. In particular, they could prove expensive in terms of specialist equipment. The argument that is said to have tipped the balance is that mini-schools will increase the attachment of each student to responsible members of staff. Both care and discipline can be tightened; two arguments, appealing in different measure to different teachers, for an action that can therefore be agreed. Common ground. The Industry Project in Cleveland (**A4**) reports similarly diverse support for a single action, different constituencies finding their own reasons for support.

ENQUIRING

Enquiring means finding out about what people know and are doing, by asking people for information about what is going on now, what resources are being used to pursue what objectives and with what effectiveness. The questionnaire at Furtherwick Park (**D2**) is used to obtain information about what colleagues are doing now to seek to meet the needs of students, as well as for acknowledgements of needs that are not being met. A major hazard for innovation in complex organizations is that any suggestion for change is likely to invade something that is already happening. The negotiation of entry for innovation into organization, it is argued in Chapter 2, requires that the current preoccupations of people are understood and their reactions can be adapted. Both require that somebody asks questions of users and audiences in the organization before things go too far. In the case of the Community Newspaper Project (**D3**) it is the spontaneous expression of concern by students which provides impetus. It is reported (Evans and Law, 1984) that information generated by such enquiry, such as that carried out in the work of the Careers Guidance Integration Project at 'Dane Park' School (**F3**), tends to be rejected if it is not produced by the people to whom it is addressed. A more basic problem might be ensuring that people know what is being produced by enquiry: one Clydebank teacher is reported thus '[. . .] we got things to fill in every other week, giving our opinions, verdicts, judgements — and nothing ever happened; no feedback'.

REQUESTING

Requesting involves people in the action, by calling on their knowledge and experience as part of a development team. Knowledge of who those people should be is, it is argued, a matter of management 'feel', by sensing who has what energy for the action. The Clydebank adviser seems to have taken that role. It is not necessarily the case that designated people from the relevant departments should be the people, certainly not the only people, to be involved. There are strong arguments for making initiatives which link people from a variety of sections and departments in any organization. The involvement of departments in the pre-vocational initiative to emerge from the survey at Furtherwick Park is remarkable for its diversity.

REFLECTING

Reflecting invites people to disclose their anticipation and, later, experience in the use of the action. Anxiety may be an early response to suggestions for innovation. Reports suggest that there is a progression through the setting up, implementation and review of most initiatives, taking time to accomplish. Attitude change, for example, is reported to be as much a consequence as a cause of involvement. Also, it is reported that disclosure of responses to the action is as likely to be effective when it is negotiated with colleagues and peers, as when it is done with designated outside consultants. A commonly reported benefit from in-service training is contact with peers.

HELPING

Helping means putting resources at the disposal of the action. In-service training is usually well jigged to show people materials and to help them develop skill and confidence in adapting and using them. The sort of feedback-on-performance and coaching mentioned in Chapter 2 are possible features of in-service training. But most in-service training can do little to improve people's position, in terms of command of role and resources in the organization, in such a way as to make their effective participation feasible.

The problems for in-service training as a major means of influencing action in schooling are, in large part, problems of re-entry (Law, 1977b). The issues dealt with in training may be the right issues, but they are not always being negotiated with all the right people. The right people include the colleagues who await, or are indifferent to, the return of the participant. Designs for in-service training increasingly incorporate provision for teams of teachers to attend courses, interleaving periods of workshop activity with consultancy-supported action in the schools, the course being used not only to develop plans for action but to anticipate and prepare for the reactions of colleagues (Law, 1984).

The importance of grass-roots reactions to innovation, and the complexity of the tasks entailed when influence on innovation is sought, both suggest that development use might be made of schooling's existing small-group staff activity. It is, or has been, a feature of schooling that a series of meetings will be held between colleagues sharing in a common task in the organization. They may be curriculum-development groups, case conferences to review student progress, monitoring groups to keep an eye on the progress of aspects of the programme and so on. In some cases they have been informal, relying on goodwill and volunteered time. Most of the tasks described above will be on the agendas of many such groups. They have the advantage of engaging a variety of personalities in development work (and the repertoire of skills and styles required for such work is sufficiently wide to suggest team rather than individual effort). Such groups are established as a result of the survey at Furtherwick Park, of the concerns addressed by the teachers who set up the Community Newspaper Project and of subgroup activity in Clydebank. Such groups are key features of the Transition to Working Life Project (**A3**) and Cleveland's Industry Project schools (**A4**); these groups have been established in such a way as to open the external boundary of the school as well as its internal boundaries.

ACTION

INFLUENCING ACTIONS

This assumes that there is something new you would like to see done or something that you would like to see done differently. A better assumption is that you are involved in this with a group. But it is not an assumption that all the members of the group are in any sense bosses. It summarizes the content of this chapter in a series of checklists for action, something which could form the basis of a contract for action between you and your partners. Very little of this work can be done by means of staff training. Most of it requires the use of existing or the establishment of new task-group activity in the organization.

WHOM SHOULD WE SEEK TO ENGAGE?

It is probable that for most proposals for action there is going to be a need to engage more than one person or group of people, so that they will help the development of the action you have in mind.

Who [. . .]	So that they will help by [. . .]

At 'Macro' level
Policy makers; readers, listeners
and viewers of national or local
media; who else?

At 'Exo' level
Constituencies and pressure groups
for employers, employees, the
churches, the unemployed,
teachers, parents, students;
who else?

At 'Meso' level
The organization or department as a
whole; other organizations; their
managers, audiences, caucuses and
grass-roots workers; who else?

At 'Micro' level
Individual users of the proposal
for new action; individual
students; who else?

HOW DO WE INTEND TO SET ABOUT IT?

Different groups require different approaches. Who can do what, with whom, to ensure the best chance of survival and implementation for the proposed new action?

Who should inform whom about what?

Who should canvass whom about what?

Who should ask whom for what information?

Who should ask, or negotiate with, whom to do what?

Who should be providing
opportunities to reflect with whom,
about what?

Who should be offering
help to whom, with what?

What else?

Different members of any group involved in the planning of this action will have different contributions to make. The examination of influencing styles invited at the beginning of the chapter is intended to suggest clues about who might best undertake what influencing action?

CHAPTER 6

EXPERIENCE-BASED LEARNING

In this chapter the following are examined critically:

- what influences people's individual pre-vocational development
- the significance of personal encounters in that process
- what methods and materials have been developed to help students gain and set down such experience-based learning.
- what to take account of in planning experience-based pre-vocational learning.

Think of a young adult known to you who has a career-development dilemma to resolve or problem to solve; a person (perhaps) not knowing what to do, or (even) what can be done, or (anyway) how to go about it. Pre-vocational education has a battery of techniques to help but, in this case, how helpful would any of them be?

'Matching' techniques seek key features in the personality of the person, compare them with key features in the opportunities being considered, so that a match can be made. They emphasize the importance of attention being paid to the free-standing individuality of the person. There are aptitude tests, career-interview schedules, paper-and-pencil interest questionnaires, self-assessment schedules, computer programs and formative profiling techniques designed to bring this person to the point where he or she might be able to say 'that's for me!'.

'Enabling' techniques provide a non-threatening space in which the person can explore the layers of individual thought and feeling attached to the situation. Techniques have been developed to enable a person in disclosing, unpicking, articulating and reordering that personal material. Counselling replaces interviewing; client-centred reviewing infuses profiling. There is also a range of group and classroom techniques setting up simulated and role-played encounters. All are meant to help a person know what his or her personal and unique response to the situation is; 'this is how I see it!'.

'Coaching' techniques help the person acquire and sharpen career-development skills, capabilities and competencies. The person might be helped, for example, by learning how to plan, to find and land a job, to present his or her self successfully to others, to be assertive, or to manage a time or money budget. In some cases models of how to do it are provided; in some cases feedback is given so that people can identify and sharpen their individual ways of going about such tasks. Terms such as social and life skills and personal effectiveness training gain currency. The successful endpoint is 'I can do that!'.

'Networking' techniques put the person into direct and personal contact with people she or he might not otherwise meet. If information is gained it will be from the testimony of people who are there. If skills are to be sharpened they will be sharpened in the situations to which they apply. If models are to be found they will be found in flesh-and-blood. If feedback is to be received it will be received from the horse's mouth. It can be implemented by bringing the contacts to the learners, but work experience arranges it by taking the learners to the contacts. Work experience is not the only technique for taking students into direct and personal contact with the people and places of which they learn. A term to refer to the whole range of techniques is experience-based learning.

You might judge that your person would gain something from each of the techniques; all are necessary, none is sufficient. Indeed the effectiveness of any one of them requires the use of others. This chapter is addressed to the necessity of experience-based learning.

ACTIVITY
AUTOBIOGRAPHICAL LINE

The autobiographical line represents the passage of some critical transition in your life (some time when you have some dilemma to resolve or some problem to solve) and sets out the beginning, middle and end of that phase (Figure 6.1). Above the line, record what you know at the time (things done, things said, places, people and whatever else constitute the features of the transition). Then mark the features that influenced you and

FIGURE 6.1   Time line for transition

This is
what
happens:

Beginning   Middle   End

This is
what is
important
to me
and why:

what you thought and felt about them. Enter below the line why they are important. It is an exercise in identifying what influences the way you deal with this dilemma or problem. It can be repeated usefully to set out more than one such transition. (An adaptation of this time–line activity can prove useful to students. This one is based on Law and Storey, 1986.)

How important is the free-standing independence of your personality and its characteristics? Or the subtle layers of thought and feeling that constitute your view of self-in-situation uniquely? Or your personal, social and career-development competencies? Or the people around you at the time?

Life is sufficiently interesting to make it certain that any analysis attempted here will not be exhaustive. But this chapter is based on the assumption that the people who are around, when we do, or do not, resolve such transitions, are significant. It is given to an examination of how people learn from such encounters and how they can be helped fruitfully to learn.

INPUT
LEARNING FROM AN EXPERIENCE BASE

Studies of career development and of the use of experience-based programmes suggests the following about what young men and women gain: they

- receive *feedback*, about what they can do and are like.
- encounter *models*, people who represent new possibilities for their own lives.
- build *impressions*, of the sight, sound and feel of new environments and relations.
- receive *support*, encouragements and support for a line of action.
- sense *expectations*, a sense of what is demanded of their own adulthood.
- make *contacts*, people who can help them find places in adult and working life directly.

Each section following is accompanied by examples of how such gains are made and illustrative quotations taken from student reports.

RECEIVING FEEDBACK

Experiences which give me new impressions of what I can do, am like and enjoy. Much of it is in the way people behave toward me. A lot of it is unintentional, a by-product of being involved in something together. Much of it is implicit rather than explicit. People are hungry for feedback; the implications are rarely missed.

- Finding myself involved in something which I can do or enjoy particularly.
- Being treated as though I am capable and motivated in a particular activity.
- Noticing something said or implied about me.

'We were [. . .] always expected to do it properly. At one point when I made a mistake

I was asked to start from the beginning again and do it properly: this wasn't checked at the end — as they trusted us.'

'I know what I can do properly now.'

'We were being treated different, in a way that we were being treated as grown ups not as school children no more.'

'All of us have matured so much through this experience. We've learned so much about ourselves and each other [. . .]. Now I know that this was part of an experience from which we've gained a lot of knowledge and maturity.'

'The woman smiled and commented on how enthusiastic I looked, how patient I looked with such a boring job.'

'The old lady took out her purse and pushed twenty pence into my hand. I could feel my cheeks burning with embarrassment but, as I thanked her, I felt so proud.'

'I was getting faster at everything at the end of the day [. . .]. I was getting more confident. Therefore I was getting bored with it. I didn't want to do anything hard [. . .]. I just wanted to get more involved.'

ENCOUNTERING MODELS

Recognition in other people of something which calls up admiration, respect or liking. It might be just an acknowledgement of a new understanding of what other people are like, but it sometimes becomes the basis for an aspiration: something that I begin to recognize in myself, want to recognize in myself or feel drawn toward. Their story somehow gives me a clue about my own story.

- Encountering lives and lifestyles different from anything properly encountered before and feeling its worthwhileness.
- Noticing that other people cope, even thrive, with qualities no more impressive than my own and seeing in that possibilities for myself.
- Finding a target group membership of which is sought, shaping my actions to make it more likely that I will gain entry; using 'people like that' as an inspiration to my own actions.

'Everyone seemed happy and friendly toward each other. I felt so out of place, like an immature kid.'

'I have seen what other people's lives are like and how they work.'

'After I heard that everyone else does the same mistakes, it made me realize I'm human too. Now I can admit mistakes which I wouldn't before I went [. . .].'

'I didn't used to talk to blokes like [. . .]; he's older than me own dad! I didn't used to know blokes like that, just kids my own age. I used to get on with him fine.'

'It was good to hear that other people were in the same boat as me. I always had the impression that it was just me the world was picking on, not anyone else.'

'Sometimes you think you are the only one in a certain situation and meeting other people in the same situation as you sort of boosts you up a bit.'

'With [. . .] you could tell that grown-up people like a laugh.'

'At work people don't divide in groups of friends like they do at school; certain people don't seem to dominate and speak for everyone as at school. I think this is because people grow up and they become less dependent on other people, and they don't feel that they have to be the same as everybody else.'

'The thing that made it better was the woman I was beside, she was very nice: always talking to me and explaining things, every question I asked she helped me by answering and telling me.'

'How skilfully she worked with her hands. I wished I was in her place. Even though I was bored I still wanted so much to have a job there and be able to wear one of the orange overalls (even though they weren't really to my liking).'

'My first day finished. It had been great. Wonderful. The staff were "canny", the clients interesting.'

RECEIVING SUPPORT

Experiences of being noticed, accepted, encouraged, even enticed, to get on with something. Sometimes the support is unconditional : 'you're okay — whatever you want to do!'. More often it is intended to shape behaviour, with the attention, encouragements and facilities being placed manipulatively to draw me toward a goal desired by others. Most often it is neither, but authentic and spontaneous, just expressing people's acknowledgement of interest in and liking for me. Without such support continued effort can entail more of a drain on self-esteem than most people can afford.

- Being welcomed by people who communicate a sense of interest in me, of wanting me to be around.
- Having people who help with planning and carrying through a plan.
- Getting a feeling from others that I matter, that my past successes are important, and my future successes are desired, by them as well as by me.

'They joked as I took off my ugly wellies and black leg warmers and I laughed, glad to be noticed.'

'Helped with encouragement.'

'More attention.'

'More personal help.'

'Helped me with my personality and the job helped me also. I think over 6 weeks I've learned a lot.'

'I felt embarrassed, and more of the staff gathered round and looked at the way my hair was cut. They laughed and joked on with me calling me "madam" and things like that. I felt great. If only I had a week left instead of a day [. . .]. I felt absolutely wonderful. They were really talking to me and giving me a chance to answer back.'

SENSING EXPECTATIONS

Sensing the requirements and demands of the people, the place and the activity. It often comes as a realization that this is not going to be as easy or, perhaps, as glamorous as I thought. It is often threatening, at first anyway. But it is not necessarily received as 'bad news' where it is accompanied by the feeling that people who know me believe I will cope. That can be exciting. There are, of course, people who have lived out much of their lives on the basis of other people's expectations of them. But there are few who do not respond positively to less manipulative communications of the message 'it's hard, but you can do it!'.

- Finding myself in a position or role which exerts pressure on me to carry it through.
- Being with people who communicate a clear sense of the values they place on 'delivering the goods'.
- Finding that people who I am working with believe that I will 'deliver the goods'.

'I thought initially it was going to be a joy ride, but obviously I was mistaken.'

'Brought me to face the facts.'

'Pushed me so it helped me to realize the importance.'

'It made me realize all the time I had wasted at school — I regret not working harder at school.'

'Time's catching up on me — I've got to do something.'

'It has shown me that people have to work hard for their money.'

'Now I know a little bit about what it's going to be like, working 5 days a week'.

'It puts you back into reality [. . .]. It's up to you to make the most of your interview. If you want the job you've got to prove it to them. I think "now you're an adult", and it gives me confidence.'

'My feet were sore. I had hardly sat down all day. But I was looking forward to tomorrow.'

BUILDING IMPRESSIONS

Gaining my own response to the sight, sound, smell and feel of a place directly through my own senses and indirectly through the disclosure of their responses by the people who are there. It is not 'information' in the sense of 'objective data', little of which, in any event, provides most people with a basis for action. Much of it is 'testimony', something known because a person has encountered and attached him or herself to it. It comes only from direct and personal contact with the place and with the people.

● Listening to people say what they know about 'being there'.
● Observing the places, the people and the reactions of the people to each other and to the place.
● Sharing in the experience of 'being there'.

'It has shown me what working life is all about.'

'Tells me what it feels like.'

'I don't think that being told or reading books about it is as good as actually going out and doing it, and feeling what it is like for yourself.'

'It made me realize what a job's all about. It's not just a hobby or anything. It's your way of being.'

'In a large office people seemed in better humour than in offices with just ones and twos.'

'I couldn't help smiling to myself. I felt I was doing something that was more like the hair-dressing profession. Instead of just passing curlers or watching. I was in contact with a client. I was part of a hair-do'.

'This showed me that the beginning and even the end wasn't as glamorous as it looked, and I was still interested. I had found my future profession.'

'Some of the men asked me if I would like a job in ship building but I said no, because it is too noisy, cold, dirty and hungry. Also some of the men push you around and tell you to do things, in which you would not really believe in doing, also I don't really like the hours'.

'This job was interesting and it shows that by making special things for the children to get them about it can help them a lot and you feel good to be able to help them.'

'The thing I like is the uniform and the hats, the hats were like the nurses wear. I would like to go back to the hospital, I really did enjoy myself.'

'The thing that really put me off about the work experience was that I was in the one office all the time; I would have preferred it to have been trying out different things in the factory.'

MAKING CONTACTS

Finding people who are already 'on the inside' and can help by smoothing my path, opening doors and speaking up for me to a place where I want to go. It may be that they want me to join them. It may be that they can speak for me to some other organization, with a bit more influence that I, and maybe even my teachers, can pull. At least they can often offer me some 'inside information' on how to approach other similar organizations.

- Finding somebody who can give me some knowledge about whether and how particular organizations go about recruiting people like me.
- Finding somebody who will take me on, or speak up for me to somebody who might take me on.
- Finding somebody who will give me a report on how I've done: one that will carry weight in similar organizations.

'Inside information — told me what interviewers found pleasing.'

'You can get a reference if you're reliable or dependable in some way.'

'The personnel officer said that if I wanted a job I'd be better off than some people and I should get my application in as soon as possible.'

'"Mrs Sinclair" I started "do you think there's a chance of a Saturday job here?" [. . .]. "Well Karen", she said "I've been really pleased with the way you've worked [. . .] as soon as there is a place I'll let you know." I was filled with hope and longing.'

'But the best thing was the boss asked us if we were 16, and that meant he was willing to take some of us on.'

Sources: student quotations from Canon, 1979; Law, 1981; Bray, 1982; Watts, 1983; Blakey, 1984; Evans and Law, 1984.

EXAMPLES
SETTING IT UP AND SETTING IT DOWN

SETTING IT UP

Methods for the setting up of experience-based learning opportunities are diverse. They will not tidy into any analysis absolutely, but the following analysis gives some impression of the range. Each type of activity emphasizes differently the opportunity to learn from contact with: *place*, 'being here'; *functions*, 'doing this' (or 'seeing this done'); *people*, 'with Nellie'.

Visits-in refers to adults-other-than-teachers in classrooms. It can be a dilute version of experience-based learning and, probably, is not experience based at all where (say) a member of the police gives a formal talk about (say) the protection of property. But if that person discloses and exchanges with students about the stresses and pleasures of being a neighbourhood copper, then that testimony offers a sense of what it is like to be there. The trial job interviews set up between students and managers in Cleveland (**A4**) and the 'TV studio' encounters built into the Working Lives Project (**A7**) are designed to release such experience-based authority.

Task projects put students into working roles in a project established from inside schooling but engaging a real task. Tasks include the setting up of a business, the carrying out and reporting of a survey on a local issue, community service and the provision of some new facility or service inside the school or college. The learning comes from the changed role relations between students and between students and teacher. They become adults-other-than-teachers to each other and the teacher becomes an adult-who-happens-to-be-a-teacher to them. The Community Newspaper Project (**D3**) is an example.

Projects-with-consultancy put students into contact with adults-other-than-teachers. They work together on a joint task, often setting up a business on capitalist or cooperative lines. The adult-other-than-teacher works with the students on the basis of his or her role in adult and working life, a mentor to the students. The Cleveland Industry Project (**A3**) makes extensive use of this technique.

Opportunist experience bases use the contacts and roles that students already have in adult working life in the community. They will have part-time jobs, their own enterprises, affiliations to clubs and societies and other direct and personal encounters with the people and places of neighbourhood life. Schooling can help them to draw learning from these experiences, much as it can with the work-experience placements it sets up for them.

Individual links are made between students and adults-other-than-teacher on the basis of specifically identified needs. The Community Contacts Directory (**C2**) is set up to improve the chances of the right links being made, with career development of students in mind.

Work experience places students in adult roles in established operations, usually commercial and industrial firms and social and health service agencies. The curriculum development at 'Cloudly' School (**B1**) is intended to prepare students for such placements. Placements in voluntary agencies are no less work experience. Work experience does not guarantee sustained contact with hosts, the observation can be limited relatively to impressions of the place, its functions and reflections by the students about individual participation in it.

Work shadowing puts students into a 'sitting by Nellie' relation with an adult-other-than-teacher, in the place where 'Nellie' does her 'work'. She is the host. 'Nellie' might be a trombonist with the band (**A1**), but she might also be engaged in any other aspect of the economic, cultural, domestic, altruistic or political life of the community. A feature of work shadowing is that it focuses student attention on a person, rather than a situation or a function.

Residential experiences of the 'outward bound' or 'field-trip' type are experience bases, in large measure because they put students into new relations with each other and with teachers. New roles make new relations, generating new learning.

Workshops take students away from school premises to share and work on perceptions of issues and problems for adulthood in the community. A specially selected adult-other-than-teacher takes responsibility for the workshops. He or she is the host. His or her personality is of critical importance to the learning. Further outwards visits can be negotiated from the workshop base. The Transition to Working Life Project (A3) is an example.

SETTING IT DOWN

Young men and women on experience-based programmes are there to learn something. There is little question, on the evidence of students' reports cited previously in this chapter, that they do. They can be asked to talk about, portray and reflect on that learning while they are in school or college. Some programmes invite students to set down their learning: in writing and in graphics.

There is the question about how good an idea it is to formalize such learning in this way. At worst it can become just another essay to write or worksheet to complete, detached by its formality from the spontaneity of the experience. The examples set out here are not presented as an encouragement to those who feel that nothing has been completed until it is written up.

They are set out not to be copied, but to be criticized, and therefore adapted and extended, rejected and replaced. In particular, the reader is invited to consider the extent to which any of them are likely to enable students to express the sort of learning excitement conveyed by some of the quotations made previously in this chapter.

For the expression of learning is an important part of learning. Being able to represent to myself what I have seen, whom I have met, what I have felt, what I have done, what I can do and what I want, all these are necessary parts of fully possessing that learning. Being able to represent it to myself is related intimately to being able to represent it to anyone else. The world belongs to the articulate.

Many of the techniques are similar to those used in recording experience and profiling. A difference is that these formats invite a full portrayal of places and other people, as well as of self. Any resulting collection could not therefore be called a profile or record of experience; the terms portfolio or personal file are better.

There are four sets of material:

● preparing material invites students to anticipate events and to consider what they might get from them
● logging material invites students to do an 'on the hoof' job of recording impressions as they go along
● reviewing material invites students to revisit the experiences imaginatively and reflect on them
● planning and negotiating material invites students to consider what difference the experience might make, to them, and in some cases, to other people.

Full examples are given in Appendix E. An analysis of their content is given following.

E1   Preparing for Experience-based Learning

Procedures and formats invite students to articulate and set down hopes, anticipations and intentions for the event. They are sometimes heavier on advice and exhortation than on invitations to students to do their own thinking.

Existing material can be analysed into the following types of cue and question:

(a) 'What kind of placement do you want?' (ordering priorities to help decisions about what kind of experience-based placement should be sought).
(b) 'It's different out there!' (anticipating a new environment).
(c) 'Write an application' (application forms or letters simulating an application for a job).
(d) 'Be ready!' (considerations of what needs to be done in order to show up in good shape for the experience).
(e) 'Watch out!' (considerations of dangers — usually physical — and how to avoid them).
(f) 'What do you want to gain?' (anticipations and intentions concerning what can be gained from the experience).

See Appendix E1, pp. 170–173.

E2   Logging Experience-based Learning

Procedures and formats invite students to maintain a record of what is happening, as it is happening, or soon afterwards.

Existing material can be analysed into the following types of cue and question:

(a) 'How did you get on in your interview?' (where an interview has been conducted to select the student for the placement).
(b) 'Make a job study' (a report on what is entailed in doing one of the observed pieces of work, usually by interviewing a worker).
(c) 'Think about the premises' (report and reflect on the locations of premises and the allocation of space).
(d) What hardware is used? (examining tools, machines, equipment used and their impact).
(e) 'Think about the organization' (examining features of the roles, rules and output of the organization).
(f) 'How safe is it?' (examining risks — usually physical — and protections).
(g) 'What are unions for?' (asking what they do and why a person would join).

(h)   'How is the outfit doing?' (portraying progress and prospects for, and in, the outfit).
(i)   'What are they looking for in their workers?' (asking what sorts of people are taken on).
(j)   'Would you need training?' (what is needed and what is offered?).
(k)   'What differences do you notice?' (identifying dissimilarities between being at school or college and being in the workplace).
(l)   'Are you enjoying it?' (inviting expressions of pleasure and pain).
(m)   'How was it today?' (inviting a day-to-day portrayal of experience, in diaries, logs, timesheets, etc.).

See Appendix E2, pp. 173–182.

E3   Reviewing Experience-based Learning

Procedures and formats invite students to articulate and set down their impressions of the experience after the event. Some formats are given to students before and during the event as an invitation to build impressions for later review.

Existing material can be analysed into the following types of cues and questions:

(a)   'Talk about it' (invitations to loosely structured portrayal so that students can say what occurs to them to say).
(b)   'What happens?' (job studies, analyses and checklists of features of working activity made in the third person and retrospectively).
(c)   'What happened to you?' ('first person' reports of experience — what was done, for how long and where).
(d)   'Draw a picture' (invitations to make graphic representations of events, places and people).
(e)   'What did it demand of you?!' (accounts of abilities required, delivered — and not delivered — by the student).
(f)   'How did you feel?' (expressions of remembered pleasure and pain).
(g)   'Talk about the people you met' (invitations to reflect on people encountered during the experience specifically).
(h)   'What have people told you about yourself?' (invitations to identify feedback from people at the workplace).
(i)   'What have you learned?' (invitations to say what new knowledge, concepts, skills, traits have been developed).
(j)   'Did you learn what you set out to learn?' (invitations to compare intentions with outcomes).
(k)   'What was new about it?' (invitations to identify what was not anticipated or intended).

(l)   'How does your experience compare with other students?' (invitations to compare experiences and learning).

Appendix E3, pp. 182–189.

E4   Negotiating and Planning from an Experience Base

Procedures and formats invite students to articulate and set down material which will inform decision making and action. The action might be their own, such as what they are going to do now. But it might be other people's, such as 'employers' who can improve the placements they offer or teachers who can improve curriculum. The leverage that existing materials give to students in negotiation with employers and teachers is very limited. But some of the cues and questions incorporated into existing material contain the bases for such negotiations; some of them might be thought to set up expectations that such negotiations will ensue.

Existing material can be analysed into the following types of cues and questions:

(a)   'How do you rate the experience?' (asking how useful it has been).
(b)   'What does the experience suggest for your time at school or college?' (identifying action that can be taken for self, with peers and with teachers).
(c)   'How are your plans shaping?' (asking what — if anything — comes out of the experience to inform personal career development.)

See Appendix E4, pp. 189–192.

The content suggested for 'setting it down' can be related to the gains analysed previously in this chapter: receiving feedback, encountering models, receiving support, sensing expectations, building impressions and making contacts. But setting it down also means other things. Students are involved in examining self, paying attention to their own thoughts and feelings as free-standing individuals. Also, they are involved in observing environments and events, paying attention to the verifiable facts of the place and its functions rather than to more subjective testimony.

In the list following items from the material in the appendices are selected. A good many of the items can lead reflection in a number of different directions. They are analysed here to indicate the sorts of reflection that they seem likely to provoke, by using the eight headings quoted following. The codes refer to the appendices (E1 preparing; E2 logging; E3 reviewing; E4 planning and negotiating).

Examining self
'How do you feel about working outdoors? [. . .] working in a large organization?'
[. . .] etc. (E1a).
'Underline the words that best describe any worries you may have' [. . .] (E1b).
'What do you want to find out?' (E1f).
'On the first day I felt [. . .]' (E2l).
'How do you feel about returning to school now your work experience is over?' (E4b).
'Has the experience helped you to make up your mind about [. . .]?' (E4c).

Receiving feedback
'After interviews most people think of better answers [. . .] write down what you think
would have been better answers' (where there is a selection interview for the placement)
(E2a).
'Was your supervisor pleased with your work? What did he/she say about it?' (E2m).
'The words underlined describe the way you go about things in this situation' [. . .] (the
student is encouraged to share the assessment with a contact on the placement) (E3h).

Encountering models
'A profile of my favourite workmate' (E2m).
'A Day in the Life of [. . .]' (essay title) (E3a).

Receiving support
'Use this page to get your workmates to write a little note to you. Stick photos of them
in if you wish.' (E2m).
'Do you find that people became friendlier [. . .]?' (E3g).

Sensing expectations
'It is expected that your project will involve: a very high level of attendance.' [. . .]
(E1d).
'What skills which are needed at work do you think should be taught at school?' (E4b).

Building impressions
'In relation to new technology [. . .] how do they feel it will affect the types of job they
are doing?' (E2d).
'Why do people join trade unions?' (E2g).
'How is work different from school?' (E2k).
'Was there anything which was said, or done, which was a surprise to you?' (E3k).

Making contacts
'Will you go back to see the people there?' (E3g).
'Did anyone in the company mention the possibility of employment in future years?'
(E3g).

Observing environments and functions
'Job interviews' (job study) (E2b).
'Which two departments take up the greatest amount of space? Why do they need so
much space?' (E2c).

'What safety rules must you follow [. . .]?' (**E2f**).
'How does the union help its members [. . .]?' (**E2g**).
'Write a short account of the history of the company [. . .]' (**E2h**).
'Does this job serve the people [. . .] directly? [. . .] indirectly? [. . .]' (**E3b**).

EXPLORATION
SECOND THOUGHTS ON EXPERIENCE-BASED LEARNING
EXPERIENCE-BASED LEARNING AS METHOD

Experience base provides a teaching-and-learning method worth comparing with other methods, such as didactic, participative and experiential methods.

Didactic method is visualized commonly as a (standing-up-talking) teacher transmitting material to (sitting-down-listening) students. The dyed-in-the-wool didactic teacher does not expect to change her or his view of the situation as a consequence of teaching. A pre-vocational technique which lends itself to didactic method is matching interviewing of the 'one-day-you'll-thank-me-for-this' type; students have been known to clutch computer print-outs with reciprocal gratitude and relief. But few teachers, and not many designers of computer programs, want such a passive response from students. There is, in most teacher–student relations, discussion of the information and concepts being transmitted. There are things that should be taught didactically because they cannot be learned in other ways (or, anyway, they cannot safely be learned in other ways).

Participative method insists that the students become active; usually, it requires that desks and chairs are moved. In, for example, coaching on what is involved in being successful in an interview, participants can simulate the actions of selector and candidate. There are pre-designed packages of participative material, such as simulations of production processes which bring students into active engagement with a representation of (say) features of line management. It is often the case in participative learning that the teacher knows in advance what he or she intends the students to learn; some problem-solving exercises are designed to lead to the discovery of the advantages of cooperative action. But, as every Nuffield science teacher knows, it does not always come out as predicted. The primary intention of participative methods is learning-by-doing. Where the objectives are for problem solving or skill acquisition then participative methods are clearly preferable. Students will be better able to understand and handle the situation because they have been engaged in acting it through.

Experiential method invites the students to become involved personally. It can happen spontaneously, where, for example, the simulation of selector and candidate call up real here-and-now feelings. But teaching-and-learning is also predesigned to enable experiential learning. An example is a role play of a contentious survival situation in which each student is asked to show what he or she would show personally and individually in that situation. Experiential method involves disclosure, the curriculum is what students say and do. For this reason, teachers cannot know in advance what each student will gain from it. There are some pre-vocational questions which have no right answers, known by the teacher in advance. Decision making is like that, because decisions call on personally and individually held feelings and values. There will be no right answer, there need be no consensus. Each student will find each her or his own learning. A primary intention of experiential methods is affective, as well as intellectual and behavioural involvement.

The distinctions made above focus on deepening levels of involvement by the student. They identify consequences for disclosure on the part of the student and for an inability to predict what will be learned on the part of the teacher. Both student and teacher are accepting more risk in participative than in didactic work and more still in experiential work. But participative and experiential learning can invade all classroom work. An alert and sensitive teacher will find him or herself working with experiential material in a lesson that was designed as didactic. The willingness of the students to disclose is as necessary to that process as is the intention of the teacher. Where students are prepared to disclose, lessons designed as didactic will be transformed; where they are not, lessons designed as experiential will be sterile.

Experience-based method calls on direct and personal contact with the object of learning. It uses the reality of which it learns. Work experience puts students into contact with the places, functioning and people of adult and working life. The examples section of this chapter lists a range of other such contacts. Some is set up by schooling, some is drawn from the warp and weft of students' experience. Some brings the experience into the classroom, some sends the students to the experience.

Experience-based learning also invades other methods. For example, role plays can engage students in action which represents an authentic part of their experience-in-the-world and, where this experience is brought into the classroom to become the material of learning, it is an experience base. Where that happens the students' experience becomes the resource; they are the adults-other-than-teachers, a fourth franchise to add to the three identified in Chapter 3. It is also based on the disclosure of 'being there' made by visitors who are prepared, not to give a formal and distant talk, but to permit encounter with their own dilemmas and concerns [like that permitted by the policeman and the toolmaker in the Working Lives Project (A7)]. Changing the role relations between students, and between students and mentors, often represents an experience base for learning, even where it is happening on site: for example, were adults-other-than-teachers act as consultants to students involved in a mini-enterprise, and in the Community Newspaper Project (D3) where the teacher becomes a consulting member of the students' enterprise.

However, the fullest experience base is found off-site, in task projects, work shadowing and work experience, which take students to learning environments in community. But distinctions at least as important as that between on-site and off-site, are those between experiences which emphasize the relative importance of contact with the place, with the functioning and with the people of the experience. The argument in the first part of this chapter is for the importance of encounters with people. Some off-site work experience offers little in this respect.

What participative, experiential and experience-based methods have in common in their insistence that the student accepts self-propelled responsibility for using teaching-

and-learning experiences actively. These methods are part of a sea change in the profession. Like programmed learning, distance learning, interactive computer-based learning, and TV- and video-based learning, they require that the teacher becomes less a lecturer and more a manager of resources and monitor of students' gains.

MONITORING, RECORDING AND NEGOTIATING

Techniques for the recording of student achievement are integral to this change, especially where they develop the role of teacher as one who sits with students at regular intervals and asks 'what do you mean to gain from this', 'what are you gaining from it?', 'what have you gained from it?' and 'what do you mean to do about it?'. The material for setting down experience-based learning set out previously in this chapter is arranged to correspond to these four student-centred reviewing questions. There has never been a time when teachers have not asked these variations on the question 'how are you getting on with this?'. The development of student-centred reviewing materials and methods supports and extends the process.

Part of the recent rhetoric for the role is that students and teachers negotiate; the possibility of negotiation is also implicit in some of the cues included in material to engage students in setting down experience-based learning. The material (particularly in E4) incorporates invitations to evaluate the placement and to consider what might be done to help students make better use of placements.

There is little point in asking such questions unless something is to be done in response; teachers, individually and as part of system, are among the people who could act on the emerging suggestions. Negotiation from an experience base transforms the last of the questions set out above to 'what can you — and what can I, and what can schooling — do about it?'. Negotiation implies flexibility on both sides; that we are prepared to do things differently. Part of the fourth franchise, students as adults-other-than-teachers, is that they will have a say in the design and implementation of their education.

RISKS IN EXPERIENCE-BASED LEARNING

Experience-based learning franchises adults-other-than-teachers in their educative work. The value students place on such encounters is reported in the input section above. But the materials developed to engage students in setting down their experiences do not always follow the students' energies in this respect. In much there is a high concentration of cues to make more-or-less objective portrayals of the situation and functioning in the placement, less to elicit the testimony of the people there.

That may be safer. For where students are encouraged in encounters with adults-other-than-teachers there is risk. Teachers must accept that things will be learned that would not, perhaps could not, be learned in schooling. They must accept that they will not be able to anticipate what students will learn. They may have to accept that they will not always approve enthusiastically what has been learned. The head in the school where plans are developed for developing a community newspaper (D3) doesn't want a project promoting the activities of anarchists, drop-outs, the CND and the NF. The careers coordinator running the Community Contacts Directory (C2) shows a similar concern, following up each contact with students to see if it has been helpful and, if there is evidence of persistent unhelpfulness, removing the card. It is a feature of networks that boundaries, which contain, retain and make safe, are breached and, once they are breached, you can never be sure who may be met and what may be said.

A low tolerance for such risks can be accommodated partly by controlling carefully the people whom students are permitted to meet. It can also be accommodated by scheduling carefully the questions which students are cued to ask. The teachers proposing the community newspaper take neither course, arguing that it is better for young men and women to come into first contact with such groups while they still have a chance to examine their ideas critically, and in a setting which contains all kinds of countervailing points of view.

But, as in other teaching-and-learning methods, the use students make of the experience is in their own control; there is therefore no total safety in experience-based learning. It requires that the adults-other-than-teachers who are franchised are trusted, that the students are trusted to be able positively to learn from whatever they find and that we trust ourselves to help them make positive use of what they find.

WHY EXPERIENCE-BASED LEARNING?

Experience-based learning responds to perceptions of students as having too little contact with adult and working lives in their communities. Some see little outside their inner-city patch. But leafy suburbs can also be ghettos. A ghetto is entrapment which does not permit an understanding of what is happening, and what might be possible, beyond earshot of a shout for a home goal at the local football ground. Most are bounded by contacts with immediate family, schooling and peer group. Some students may even have difficulty in giving a sustained account of what members of their own families do for a living. Isolation from all except people born within a year-or-so of 'my generation', an age ghetto, is a mentality with which the media, and much schooling, colludes. Perceptions of what happens outside those boundaries are, too often, composed of stereotypes.

'Why', it has been asked, 'do we offer work-experience placements to students who we know stand little chance of gaining work like that when they are finished with schooling?'. 'Is it not cruelly misleading to lead them all to expect something which we know we can offer only to some?'. The questions have compelling force in many parts of the country. Yet if we permit lives to develop with no contact with the way in which a good many people make their living, we are confirming them in a marginal position: reinforcing the boundaries of the ghetto.

In any event work experience is but one form of experience-based learning. Franchising activity can be extended to make contacts with a much fuller range of working activities (A5, A7, B2, C2, C3 and D3).

A rationale for experience-based learning is, then, that students be attached to their community. An assumption of the Transition to Working Life Project (A3) is that young men and women have the capabilities of adulthood; they do not need to be taught anything, they need settings in which they can become aware of their capabilities to be adult. These capabilities, it is argued, are best released in encounters with ordinary people in natural relations. There is a rationale for what might be called the invasion of the youth ghetto, pressing on young men and women attachments to the society of which they are members, and for the development of which ultimately they, not we, must accept responsibility.

THEORETICAL JUSTIFICATION

Arguments that experience-based learning makes for more self-propelled students and attaches students more extensively to their community are, in part anyway, ideological (and none-the-worse for that). But there is also a theoretical justification.

There has been a debate between career-development theorists. On the one hand, there are those who argue that the choices and transitions which constitute career development are best understood in psychological terms, because they entail the implementation of self as a free-standing and independent individual (Daws, 1977). On the other hand, there are those who argue that sociological terms are more relevant, because people are carried to their career destinies by the vortices of what is, and is not, available in the opportunity structure and by the currents of upbringing which may, but usually do not, lead them to a choice in the matter (Roberts, 1981).

The analysis of cues to students, given previously in this chapter, reflects this polarization of views. It begins with invitations to more introspective reflection and moves toward invitations to make more objective accounts of external circumstances and events. The middle part of the analysis is given to cues which invite students to learn from encounters. Gaining feedback, models, impressions, support, expectations and contacts, all these require that the student meets somebody.

The analysis is based on a review of theoretical and research work, leading to a conclusion that it is to these community interactions that student attention most naturally turns. It is neither psychological nor sociological in emphasis, but, if anything, social–psychological. It supports, moreover, the contention that where those networks of encounters can be extended beyond the people that students habitually meet, then the options that they begin to consider are extended correspondingly. Reports of various studies included in the review suggests that such extended contacts can help students to become more purposeful, more striving, more assertive, more exploratory, more informed with alternatives and less anxious (Law, 1981, 1982).

Evaluations specifically of work experience report a range of verifiable gains, including gains on such criteria as student motivation, social and educational development, knowledge and understanding of self, knowledge and understanding of society, vocational development and anticipatory effects. They report some, not always great, improvement in job knowledge, commitment to industry, a more informed view of industry and trades unions and a greater likelihood of being employed on leaving school. But the same source also cites subjective studies which give voice to student's own perceptions of what they gain. That voice contains a high concentration of reports of the value of people encountered (Watts, 1983).

Reviews made of the impact of experience-based learning reported in this book elaborates the picture. The Parkway Project's teachers (**A2**) claim that their students mature more rapidly than in conventional schooling. City-as-school (**A2**) claims that its programme has led to improved attendance, course completion, career-education competencies, self-awareness and positive attitudes to school. When asked to assess the impact of the Transition to Working Life workshops (**A3**) tutors in the schools report that no student shows evidence of negative change and that around 70 per cent show evidence of positive change (in maturity, self-confidence, approach to school work and making future options). An evaluation of pilot workshops claims that more than half of the participants show clear evidence of having 'taken responsibilities for themselves in tackling their situation'. In Cleveland (**A4**) it is claimed that students have been helped to enlarge their horizons, become more confident, learn about things the teachers don't know and have 'a new maturity in complaint'. Attendance is also reported to have improved; teacher–student relations are reported to have become more mutually confident and respecting.

A theoretical rationale for experience-based learning is, then, that the extended range of personal encounters it requires is an important resource for career-development learning. There is not enough to be learned about 'being there with them' by 'sitting here by ourselves'.

ACTION

A DESIGN SPECIFICATION FOR EXPERIENCE-BASED LEARNING

The list of issues set out below summarizes this chapter and invites answers to questions which will yield a design specification for an experience-based learning programme. A design specification is a list of the factors to be taken into account in the development of a new product. It stops short of making operational suggestions for specific actions. It is a useful device where any complicated undertaking is in hand; production of a list of detailed operational suggestions, for specific activity, people and materials, can be a hiding-to-nothing. It invites what often proves to be argumentative attention to operational detail before underlying issues have been clarified and agreed properly.

A design specification can be used as a way to review existing activity, with a view to its re-design. It can be a useful document to canvass with users, clients and audiences, before any detailed proposals are made. Indeed once the design specification has been agreed it will be surprising if users, clients and audiences cannot make their own suggestions about how it can be achieved operationally. The specification issues that emerge from this chapter include those for the following.

- *Intentions* that can range from intending that students gain specific learning (verifiable knowledge, appropriate skill, suitable attitude) to an intention that students will realize their own attachments to the people and places of the society in which they have adult membership.
- *Objectives* that can be linked to matching objectives (students will be able to say 'that's for me' or '[. . .] not for me'), through enabling objectives (students will take possession of and articulate their own personal thoughts and feelings about

themselves and working life), to coaching objectives (they will learn how to handle themselves in working environments).

- *Contacts* that can range from experience-based contacts with each other and with their teachers, through contacts with management in industry and commerce, to ordinary working people and people engaged in a wide range of cultural, media, voluntary, social and political enterprise offering wider conceptions of work.
- *Settings* that can range from visits-in, through schooling-based task projects and the opportunistic use of student's warp-and-weft experience in community, to work shadowing, a week-or-more of placement in an established work setting off-site, sustained off-site contacts with working coaches and residential experiences.
- *Roles of adults-other-than-teachers* that can range from visiting speaker (mentor) through co-worker with students (mate), consultant to students in a project, to 'Nellie's role' of friend and focus and to manager of students' learning in the workshop or workplace.
- *Support* that harnesses the techniques of classroom-based work and counselling and which can be set up to ensure that students know what they intend to gain from the experience base, what they are gaining from it, what they have gained from it and what they intend to do about it.
- *Negotiation* (of action) that can range from decisions which students might take from an experience base, through decisions which teachers might take in response to the learning students report, to adjustments to the curriculum and organization of the schooling system which responds to new needs they identify.
- *Materials* that, if they are to be used, can lead to the development by students of a portfolio of learning which can invite different attention to be paid to the structure, function and people of the experience base and which can be adopted from existing material, but which should be adapted from that material or created by the development team.

The issues are interdependent. Resolution of one will enable resolution of others. Resolution of all will begin to identify necessary operational details: for example, concerning whether work experience should be a sustained contact with one workplace, or whether it should provide for a taste of a number of different situations.

CHAPTER 7

USERS, CONTRIBUTORS AND AUDIENCES

In this chapter the following are examined critically:

- attitudes that may support or oppose community-linked pre-vocational activity
- how networks develop their franchise, from stage to stage
- skills used to support participation
- decisions about what to do next in any continuing situation.

You may find Professor Ted Wragg's analysis of responses to proposals for innovation recognizable from your own experience. Wragg assigns each ploy a 'drag coefficient': a quantification of the degree of its resistance to change. For example, the 'we've tried it already' ploy is about twice as efficient in opposing newcomers as in opposing experienced teachers. The explanation of its usefulness lies in the fact that it causes proposers of new action to feel that it is they who are naive and out-of-touch. The 'there's no demand for it' ploy is, however, less efficient largely, Wragg argues, because it implies an unsupportable assumption that education is articulated to consumer demand.

Use of the 'it's the wrong time' ploy is more hopeful because it suggests that the proposer has missed his or her golden opportunity or, better still, that postponement is the only rational response (leaving the opposer in the declared position of basic support for the proposal). The efficiency of the ploy 'people won't like it' varies with whom the people are thought to be. 'Parents won't like it' is more efficient than 'the community won't like it' because, in the latter case, nobody knows precisely whose disapproval they may be risking. Where, however, the ploy is used in the form 'the boss won't like it' the drag coefficient takes on a negative value, guaranteeing general approval for the proposed action. Wragg, rather subtly, suggested that this may be exactly the way in which some devious bosses have gained support for preferred action.

The professor proposes the formation of a Society of Logjammers, Obstructionists, Thwarters and Hinderers (an acronym will, of course, have to be found) to provide a forum for the dissemination of his Taxonomy of Educational Obstruction (Wragg,

1984). Although a trailblazing piece of work, Wragg's analysis merely identifies the superficial social and life skills of obstruction; it pays little attention to its underlying purposes, other than by referring to the sorts of arbitrary rationalization that people drag in. Even where such arguments can, at first, be counterpoised, the opposing purpose is likely to remain, perhaps to reassert later.

ACTIVITY

LINKING ATTITUDES AND UNLINKING ONES

The problem is therefore not only that people may prevent the pre-vocational franchise, but that they may, subsequently, seek to subvert or hijack it for their own purposes. Conflict may precede implementation, but it may also come to the boil during implementation. Statements of attitude to pre-vocational links are given in Figure 7.1. They set up a scale, not to yield a reliable drag coefficient, but to provide a tool by means of which you can examine your own attitudes and compare them with other people's.

Each of the statements completes the sentence 'The pre-vocational franchise is important for its capacity to [. . .]'. What priority do you give to each? Your first gut reaction

FIGURE 7.1   Statements of attitude to pre-vocational links

The pre-vocational franchise is important for its capacity [. . .]

		+3	+2	+1	0	−1	−2	−3	
1	[. . .] to bring in a variety of new perspectives and thinking.	1	2	3	4	5	6	7	C
2	[. . .] to qualify for additional government funding.	7	6	5	4	3	2	1	C
3	[. . .] to give the grass roots a forum for a voice in the politics of education.	1	2	3	4	5	6	7	A
4	[. . .] to bring schooling into accountable line with mainstream policy making.	7	6	5	4	3	2	1	A
5	[. . .] to introduce students to alternatives to conventional paid employment.	1	2	3	4	5	6	7	B
6	[. . .] to invite local people and organizations to help with resources.	7	6	5	4	3	2	1	C

(Continued)

FIGURE 7.1   (*Continued*)

7	[. . .] to give individual students more resources and perspectives than can otherwise be found.	+3 / 1	+2 / 2	+1 / 3	0 / 4	-1 / 5	-2 / 6	-1 / 7	E
8	[. . .] to improve the employability of young men and women.	+3 / 7	+2 / 6	+1 / 5	0 / 4	-1 / 3	-2 / 2	-3 / 1	B
9	[. . .] to support the teacher's new role as resource manager for self-propelled learning.	+3 / 1	+2 / 2	+1 / 3	0 / 4	-1 / 5	-2 / 6	-3 / 7	C
10	[. . .] to respond to legitimate pressure to relate schooling to society's needs.	+3 / 7	+2 / 6	+1 / 5	0 / 4	-1 / 3	-2 / 2	-3 / 1	E
11	[. . .] to counterpoise centrist power with what local and grass-roots people know.	+3 / 1	+2 / 2	+1 / 3	0 / 4	-1 / 5	-2 / 6	-3 / 7	A
12	[. . .] to attach students more firmly to the values of industry and commerce.	+3 / 7	+2 / 6	+1 / 5	0 / 4	-1 / 3	-2 / 2	-3 / 1	DE
13	[. . .] to inform the imagination of students, so they can create new futures.	+3 / 1	+2 / 2	+1 / 3	0 / 4	-1 / 5	-2 / 6	-3 / 7	BE
14	[. . .] to use the authoritative thinking of leaders in pre-vocational education.	+3 / 7	+2 / 6	+1 / 5	0 / 4	-1 / 3	-2 / 2	-3 / 1	A
15	[. . .] to put students where they learn effectively to challenge and change things.	+3 / 1	+2 / 2	+1 / 3	0 / 4	-1 / 5	-2 / 6	-3 / 7	D
16	[. . .] to help students know what to expect of employment and what it expects of them.	+3 / 7	+2 / 6	+1 / 5	0 / 4	-1 / 3	-2 / 2	-3 / 1	D
17	[. . .] to offer schooling's plant, equipment and personnel to support new developments.	+3 / 1	+2 / 2	+1 / 3	0 / 4	-1 / 5	-2 / 6	-3 / 7	D
18	[. . .] to establish closer cooperation between schooling and industry and commerce.	+3 / 7	+2 / 6	+1 / 5	0 / 4	-1 / 3	-2 / 2	-3 / 1	B

is probably the one to pay attention to. Circle the response that most closely reflects your reaction; for the time being ignore the scores (1–7) and the boxes on the right: + 3 top priority (nothing more important); + 2 high priority (little of more importance); + 1 important (but not an overriding consideration); 0 of uncertain importance; – 1 worth some consideration (but not much); – 2 hardly worth considering; – 3 of absolutely no importance.

The issues contained in these items are intended primarily to stimulate reflection in you and discussion with partners. But they can also be scored, which can give a rough-and-ready basis for comparison of different people's and groups' positions. There is a basic score and series of cluster scores.

Basic score. Each response scores between 1 and 7. Write your scores for each item in the box on the right and total them. You will get a total of between 18 and 126.

20	30	40	50	60	70	80	90	100	110	120

- Plot M for your score, two Rs for the range of scores in the group and A for the average in the group.

Whole total: low and high system orientation

- Lower-than-average scores suggest a relative preference for strengthening schooling by diversifying its contacts, activities and interests, with alternatives to established thinking and practice.
- Higher-than-average scores suggest a relative preference for strengthening schooling by attaching it more firmly to established, consensual and policy-supported interests in education and the social system.

Cluster scores. There are five clusters of items, each representing a different emphasis in the issues. Each cluster has four items, yielding a score of between 4 and 28. The score boxes have been marked with the letters which identify each cluster.

A box total: bottom-up and top-down

5	10	15	20	25

- Lower scores envisage community links as bringing schooling into initiatives on the basis of local and grass-roots authority.
- Higher scores suggest that community links will make schooling properly responsive to policy and authoritative pressure.

B box total: wider conceptions of work and employment

5	10	15	20	25

- Lower scores envisage the need to link students to alternatives to paid employment.
- Higher scores emphasize the importance to students of gaining entry to conventional paid employment.

C box total: reform and resources in education

5	10	15	20	25

- Lower scores see community links in terms of their capacity to reform the kinds of services offered further.
- Higher scores see community links in terms of improved resources.

D box total: reform and status quo in society

5	10	15	20	25

- Lower scores see community links as part of a process of general social reform.
- Higher scores see community links in terms of supporting a traditional vision of society.

E box total: individual needs and social needs

5	10	15	20	25

- Lower scores emphasize the importance of responses to the needs of individual students.
- Higher scores emphasize the importance of responses to the needs of society.

Comparing your own cluster scores may suggest that some aspects of the issues are more important to you than others. There are no correct positions on any of the issues. They are a matter of ideological commitment and decision making. But comparing positions on these issues may identify actual or potential conflicts. Actually, none of the positions included in the items necessarily excludes any of the others. But, you may discover, people tend to favour some positions more than others.

The questionnaire can be completed usefully at the beginning and the end of some staff-development events, to see what individual and group changes have occurred.

INPUT

CHANGE 'ON THE HOOF'

Change rarely happens from a standing start. Something will have happened already, or be happening now, which will influence what can and should be done next. A great deal of what happens 'on the hoof' modifies thinking, reshapes action and gives rise to un-anticipated intentions and consequences. Managing change is therefore a matter of understanding and responding to what has and has not been resolved and to what is and what is not being resolved. It is a matter for vigilance and flexibility. Experience of school- and community-linked change suggests that vigilance and flexibility can be exercised usefully in the following areas.

DEVELOPING INTENTIONS

Questions for intent are those which journalists ask: 'What?', 'Why?', 'When?', 'How?', 'Where?' and 'Who?'. Action can falter because the people involved do not know enough about: *what* new thing is to be done; *why* it is thought worthwhile; *when*, and with what demands on time, it is to occur; *how*, and with what demands on skill and resource, it is to be carried out; *where* and with what boundaries to the action, it is to be located; *who* is interested and who is involved.

They are questions the answers to which give people a sense of the direction in which the operation is to move. Where they are not answered people tend to reduce their commitment or withdraw (psychologically or physically). The successful development of intentions usually moves from general design considerations to operational detail in a continuous process of negotiation and renegotiation with the people involved.

GETTING RESOURCES

Questions for resources are the *material*, *people* and *places* that are going to contribute to the work: 'How many?', 'How much?' and 'For how long?'. Clearly, action can falter because it is under-resourced, although committed people have achieved a great deal on a shoe-string, with a basis in goodwill that those with resource clout have no right to expect.

Action is influenced from the type as well as the quantity of resources. Particular actions may be undertaken because appropriate material for those actions is available. The direction of action is influenced by the people who join in. Action that is not possible in one place is sometimes possible in another.

In general, the more diverse the resources, the more diverse the possibility for action. Where novel and lateral thinking is the key to development the diversity of resources may be just as significant as the quantity of resources. Successful management will optimize the operation on the basis of skilful enlistment of diversity and quantity of resources.

COORDINATING RESOURCES

Questions for coordination are: 'Does the left hand of the operation know what the right hand is doing?', 'Where are the gaps in provisions?', 'How can they be filled?' and 'How can the total operation be made visible and acceptable to itself and to others?'.

Among the people involved are: *promoters*, seeking to bring the action about; *users*, expected to contribute to the action; *clients*, expected to benefit from it; *constituents*, outside the group involved directly, but represented by people in it, and whose interests are affected by what is happening; *audiences*, other people with an interest in the action.

Presumably, the promoters have a coherent view of how the parts coordinate into a whole. But clients do not always get a chance to see the programme as a whole. Users cannot always see how their contributions fit to and complement others' contributions (particularly where they are working in different departments or sectors of a widely dispersed network operation; interested audiences do not always get a clear view of the operation which is recognizable and coherent).

Successful coordination allows the left hand to know what the right hand is doing, identifies where gaps are and how they can be filled, and makes the total operation visible as coherent and acceptable to its clients and audiences.

OPENING BOUNDARIES

Questions for the opening of boundaries are about how the different perspectives in the operation can be used to cross-fertilize it, without tearing it apart: 'Where and what are the differences?', 'Are they and how are they, in conflict?', 'How can such differences be made the basis of existing activity?', 'How can they be made the basis for new activity?'. In general, the more diverse the people involved the more pressing are those questions.

Opening of boundaries identifies *differences*. It welcomes new perspectives on familiar situations. It means, for example, that people in one part of the partnership will hear what others say about what they are doing. Opening boundaries invites *conflict*. Different views are not guaranteed to be welcome and if they are not defence lines can be drawn and counter-attacks can be mounted. Also, opening of boundaries aims for *resolution*, which does not necessarily mean that everybody agrees with everything that is said, but that common ground for action is found. The point of the process is that it will yield *new bases for action*; it is the resistance of tunnel vision, the organization of lateral thinking.

A first sign that differences are beginning to poke through the boundaries is when blame begins to be attributed. The temptation to restore order by minimizing such differences is strong. At early stages that may be wise, but the confrontation of differences cannot be postponed indefinitely, if the group is to make full use of all its potential.

Sometimes caucuses form (alliances of common interest which exercise pressure on the operation) often on behalf of constituents. Where such caucuses are successful the whole operation can be hijacked in the interests of one set of interests. Where such caucuses are unremitting the whole operation can fall apart under the strain. Some groups of contributors to the action may be in a better position to form influential caucuses than others, because they have institutional back-up which gives them more clout in the operation.

The successful management of boundaries involves giving all (not just the powerful) participants a voice, allowing diversity to become visible and fruitful and being able to accept the conflict (and sometimes hostility) that is entailed.

DEVELOPING ACTION

Questions for action are about how the operation delivers anything of any use to anybody: 'What is there any justification to try?', 'Who is in the best position to do what about it?', 'What are its affects?', 'How should it be adjusted in the light of experience?'. They are all questions that seek a balance between *rationale* and *activity*, knowing why and knowing how.

A test for school–community linked partnership is 'Can it lead to justifiable action?'. The irony is that action can sometimes come too little and too late, and also too much too soon. People can be frustrated by lack of action. They can also feel rushed into action. Too much development of rationale leads to charges of talking shop; too little leads to token participation or outright rejection.

In some cases the development of a rationale for action is made a part of the action: where, for example, enquiries are undertaken into client needs and the resources that can be made available to meet those needs. Sometimes the review of rationale is built into the process of development of action: where, for example, pilot and trial actions are tried out and reviewed before full-scale implementation is undertaken. Development of rationale is also sought from evaluation and assessment procedures built into the design of full-scale action.

EXAMPLES

SUPPORTING PARTICIPATION

Accounts of pre-vocational networking activity in which attention has been paid to how members of the network engage in its work are given in the following pages. They are analysed to highlight the steps of development just described: development of intentions, how to get resources, coordination of resources, how to open boundaries and development of action. But they are analysed also in another way. The accounts indicate methods to support the participation of members of the network (see Table 7.1).

These methods, first described in Chapter 5, are:

- informing
- canvassing
- enquiring
- requesting
- reflecting
- helping.

There are cases where the work has been to make sure that all who need to know do know about what is being proposed and what is being done. They are coded *informing*.

There are cases where progress has been sought by trawling contacts, orally and in writing, for reactions and support. These attempts at taking the 'temperature' of opinion are coded *canvassing*.

In some cases contacts have been asked, formally or informally, for information,

TABLE 7.1 Supporting participation: examples of stages and methods

| Methods | Stages | | | | |
	Developing intentions	Getting resources	Coordinating resources	Opening boundaries	Developing action
Informing		F3	F1, F2		
Canvassing	F2, F3	F1, F2		F1, F3	F1, F2
Fnquiring	F1		F2, F3		F1, F2, F3
Requesting		F1, F2, F3			F2
Reflecting			F1, F2, F3	F1, F2, F3	F3
Helping	F3		F2, F3		F3

impressions, suggestions and views from contacts in the network. Such action is coded *enquiring*.

Contacts are asked tangibly to assist. Where people are being invited to contribute time, material or money in this way entries are coded *requesting*.

In some cases people have an opportunity to reflect on and explore their involvement, with whatever reactions, doubts, conflicts and suggestions for change may be entailed in that process. This is coded *reflecting*.

Cases occur where the participation is supported by help offered to network members. The help can be materials, training, consultancy, money and so on. This is coded *helping*.

The table indicates where reference is made to the use of what methods to negotiate what stages of development. It implies questions concerning what methods are appropriate to what stages of development and how development can be enhanced by adaptive use of appropriate methods at each stage. One possible use of the accounts is therefore to consider what might have happened if different methods had been used at critical points.

F1   'Elin' School–Community Group

An originating group sets up a day consultation in which a wide range of community contacts make suggestions for how careers education can be helped by members of the community. A government-funded action–research project is established to research student experience of transition from school to working life and to catalyse new action. The research identifies difficulties for students — mainly with careers education in schools, but also partly with help available while they are at work.

ACTION	EARLIER ACTION	LATER ACTION
Developing intentions	Generally to foster school–community-linked careers-education activity in the city, in particular to gain funding for the action–research project based on three schools.	As research activity starts, the group becomes interested in the more specific tasks of refining the methodology and awaiting the findings of research.
Getting resources	An originating group comprises college, school, church and careers service representatives.	An industrial manager is co-opted. Other attempts to augment the group fail — invited people argue lack of time or simply fail to turn up.
	An early day consultation canvasses a wider network of potential help. The group does not have the administrative resources to take up the variety of offers made.	The funded project provides a full-time research officer, a part-time development officer and a secretary.

Coordinating resources	Making the project more visible, through the media, is an early decision.	A suggestion that a collated account of all relevant community resources is published is thought to be more appropriate to the local careers association, and dropped.	
Opening boundaries	Early meetings are critical of the world of employment — not yet represented on the group.	School representatives express nervousness about pressure on them, which lacks an appreciation of what they are doing already.	The industrial manager hotly disputes the research findings and produces his own alternative paper on behalf of industry.

Developing action		
	The group is the sponsor and monitor of the research project into the use students are able to make of the help they are offered in their schools.	Suggestions that community links should be established in each of the participating schools founder on the argument that schools are not the most appropriate hosts to such action — because of their temporary link to students and because students might be hostile to school.
	Suggestions about recruiting community help founder on the absence of enough community representatives with whom to negotiate possibilities.	

The college appoints part-time consultants to work with teachers in the three schools and the development officer reports their work to the group. The research officer assists in the design and development of a community-linked day consultation in one of the schools and the group discusses and supports this. But these are, essentially, school-based actions and do not become part of the action to involve city-wide community resources in the terms conceived initially by the project.

No further decisions and actions are recorded in the accounts of the group's meetings.

Source: Roberts and Law, 1985.

F2   Local Liaison Groups in County Clare

The groups are set up by a European Community-funded curriculum development project — the Shannon Project for Relevant Adult Learning (SPIRAL) — working with a number of schools throughout the county. An important part of SPIRAL thinking is for the establishment of direct and personal learning contacts for students in the community. Liaison groups are established in each town — usually, in contact with more than one school — and comprise representatives from the home life, working life and educational life of each area.

ACTION	EARLIER ACTION	LATER ACTION
Developing intentions	The groups will provide community contacts for SPIRAL's community-based learning programmes, and to consult on the development of its materials.	Thinking 'flounders' for a time; groups ask the project staff, 'what do you want us to do next'. Project staff decline to direct the groups. New intentions emerge: they include a wider range of specific actions than evisaged by SPIRAL, some to be undertaken independently of the schools.

Getting resources		
Original members are local 'worthies', often already with too much on their plates.	The project assigns a consultant to the groups — to feedback impressions and catalyse new action.	Town-centre sites are found for walk-in services in one of the areas.
One school-based group quickly develops three levels of involvement: a wider network of volunteers, a series of specific task groups for particular purposes and a core group managing the whole.	Eventually, all groups seek to recruit ordinary people representing a genuine cross-section of community life, based on a community profile for each town drawn up by the consultant.	

Coordinating resources	Consultants work to make the rationale for SPIRAL more comprehensive and to help members of different caucuses more visible to, and understood by, each other.	Groups seek contact with each other to cross-fertilize thought. Groups seek a more public image in their communities.
Opening boundaries	Members of group identify differences between different representations on the group. Industrial and commercial representations are frustrated by delayed action. Teachers are cautious. Parents are diffident. As the impact of different pre-occupations, styles and back-up is realized the groups take limited steps to acknowledge conflicts.	

Developing action	Groups find community-based learning experiences for students.	Groups influence employer and trade-union recruitment policies.	A walk-in service for disaffected youngsters is established in a town centre.
	Members assess student competencies.	They research provisions and needs in the communities.	
	Members consult with teachers on programme development.	Subgroups develop a series of teaching modules on, e.g., the use of leisure.	

Although not a design specification of the project, liaison groups become an important part of its reported activity, said to be the most demanding aspect of its work. In addition to the consultant a full-time research worker is assigned to report their work.

Sources: SPIRAL, 1982; Callan and Gleeson (undated); members of Shannon, Limerick, Ennis and Kilrush Local Liaison Groups.

F3   The Careers Guidance Integration Project at 'Dane Park' School

CGIP is a government-funded action–research project interested in cross-curricular and community-linked approaches to careers education. The project, based in a polytechnic, is invited to the school and negotiates enquiry, staff and curriculum-development contracts progressively with the school over a period of 2 years. The project retains its commitment to catalysing cross-curricular and community-linked activity, but seeks common ground between this agenda and concerns expressed, at various stages, in the school.

ACTION	EARLIER ACTION	LATER ACTION
Developing intentions	There are initial doubts about how far careers can be a justifiable focus in an area of high school-leaving unemployment.	The intention becomes to extend the current level of careers guidance activity — to involve more of the social-education and pastoral-care programme. Staff- and organization-development workshops are established and the project is contracted to run them.
	An early intention is therefore for the project to review and report needs and activity in the school — taken from student and staff perceptions.	

Getting resources

A deputy head hosts the project to the school, arranging contacts and providing for the release of teachers.

Finding time for the meetings and workshops inconveniences a large number of people in the school; it is judged that there is enough understanding of and commitment to the initiative to justify the inconvenience.

The workshops are run in part on the basis of examining and trying out materials and methods.

Coordinating resources

The project team meet the whole staff before work commences — and describes its rationale and methods. All project reports are made available to the whole staff.

Later the development teams become concerned to let the whole staff know what they are doing.

A half-day consultation takes the form of an information exchange between the development teams and other colleagues in the school.

Opening boundaries	There is a school-management structure that requires team-based planning of work in open discussion. The head invites the project in without pre-empting staff reactions. Further admissions are negotiated with senior staff, the whole staff and development teams for social education and pastoral care. The careers teachers offer no resistance.		The development teams, later, acknowledge their need of help from learning resources outside the school, and to communicate what they are doing to parents.
Developing action	A survey of students' needs and available resources is carried out on behalf of the school by the project team. It leads to a suggestion — first made by the deputy head — to release more time for careers education.	Careers-education lessons are designed and delivered in the third, fourth and fifth years; there is a shift of concern toward facilitating participation by students.	Work is begun on identifying future sources of outside help which can be invited to help in classroom work.

As the aims and methods of careers education are examined in the workshops it elicits the response that much fourth-year social education and fifth-year tutorial work has been 'doing careers education' without giving it that name. The group's work becomes strengthening the career relevance of the programmes and experimenting with more participative methods. The project's interest in community-linked activity is shelved in favour of strengthening inside-the-school networks and ensuring that students recognize the relation between 'being here' (in school) and 'being there' (in adult life). The team's report notes that after a while, both the deputy head's hosting role and the project team's chairing role are taken over by the school-based team coordinators.

Source: Evans and Law, 1984.

EXPLORATION

SECOND THOUGHTS ON PARTICIPATION

A NATURAL HISTORY FOR NETWORKS?

Organisms mature in a way which should not arbitrarily be over-accelerated. They require that time and attention is paid to their needs, at all the stages of their development. The description of 'on the hoof' tasks given previously in this chapter suggest that there is a natural history of community-linked schooling, with identifiable phases, each requiring vigilant management.

Earlier phases include identifying intentions with sufficient clarity that people know what they are getting themselves into. Resources need to be found and enlisted to the action. Diversity and dispersion will, eventually, raise issues for coordination so that the operation is visible to itself, the various contributions can be related to a coherent whole, which can be made visible and recognizable to clients and audiences. Diversity of membership makes it likely that sooner or later disagreements will emerge (and conflicts). The right action at the wrong time is the wrong action.

No innovation in schooling is merely a matter of identification of an action, the design, resourcing and implementation of it and watching for how it comes out, least of all community-linked innovation. At every stage there are adjustments to be made. Yet 'there is a singular lack of curiosity about what happened to an innovation between the time it was designed and various people agreed to carry it out, and the time the consequences became evident; once an innovation was planned and adopted, interest tended to shift towards monitoring outcomes' (Fullan and Pomfret, 1977).

The unfolding of the action is a phenomenon of innovation in its own right. Descriptions of that unfolding suggest that action can get bogged down because something that should have been done earlier hasn't been done or because unnecessary agonizing over preparatory work is frustrating the participants (Roberts and Law, 1985). The 'wrong time' for the 'right action' can be both 'too soon' and 'too late'.

INTENTIONS AND RESOURCES

So, groups that fail to identify recognizable intentions at an early stage run the risk of defaulting to a 'talking shop'. By the end of the third meeting of the 'Elin' Group (E1) the chairperson is expressing frustration that the group is not concerning itself with 'the development of community resources' and regretting its feeling that 'decision on action should await research findings'. The notion of 'developing community resources' proves, in any event, pretty vague, giving very little idea of what kind of people are to be involved, on what kind of basis, to do what. An initial consultation to recruit community contacts has promised help but, when somebody on the group suggests that the group should 'tell the community what it hopes from them', members feel that they do not yet know what to ask for. The group turns to monitoring the research, in which many of its members have a natural and understandable interest because it is in their schools.

Intentions can, of course, be changed. Community-based education is an initial intention of the SPIRAL project in County Clare (**E2**); they are developed in some detail at an early stage, providing for strategies called careers explorations and learning ventures. But the liaison groups are not an original design feature of SPIRAL. They emerge from a meeting between the project director and local trades unionists, leading to an agreement to provide for direct observation of trade union–employer negotiations by students. It is the ease with which this potentially explosive exercise is carried through which causes the project team to retrace their steps in designing the project and consider how the idea of recruiting other contacts can be built into action.

Resources enlisted originally can be diversified at later stages. At first the key people recruited to County Clare's liaison groups prove to be, too dominantly, habitual members of the various committees in the community. They are too busy to give sufficient time to tightly focused and action-directed planning. One of the project consultants draws up a community profile for the neighbourhood, showing what kind of neighbourhood it is that the group is representing. This provides a basis for inviting in new people, representing aspects of ordinary adult and working life in the neighbourhood: a diversification of its resources carried out with benefit of experience. In these ways the SPIRAL project team is shown to be capable of rethinking and taking corrective action. Sometimes the best route forward is back.

COORDINATION AND CONFLICT

Action can bite off more than it can chew; too much, too soon. In one of the areas in County Clare an initial meeting attracts 300 people and trawls offers of help from 80. Not everybody regards him or herself as a member of a liaison group. But there is a great deal of goodwill. The school principal expresses delight at the range of people who have offered help, particularly when many are not the people who take part in formal meetings about schooling habitually. The school identifies three levels of involvement. A *core group* will manage the overall strategy, delegating to *task groups* specific subtasks. The bulk of contacts are thought of as *volunteers*, people who will help in whatever ways are suggested by the school, its core group or any of its task groups. One of the teachers reports later that she keeps bumping into members of the volunteer network, who ask 'do you want me yet?'. 'It is', she says, 'difficult to coordinate so much goodwill into urgent action'. This group proves to be the first in the county to cease operating. Its organization into core, task and network members may or may not have proved to be sound, but there is a doubt about whether so much diversity can be brought into mutually visible and useful action.

Conflict, where it emerges, is identifiable in a variety of ways. There are, in the County Clare liaison groups (**E2**), differences of style. An industrial representative comments on the reluctance of teachers to drive a point home, whereas teachers note the more-active less-resigned style of commercial and industrial representatives.

There are parallel differences in the content of arguments. Non-teacher members of the group are reluctant to challenge the right of teachers to be experts in their own fields. Teachers express unease about giving people ideas about changing schools. Industrial and commercial representatives express doubts about the possibility of changing a system contained by examination and professional constraint. At the same time they want to argue for the improvement of the image of manufacturing industry. Meetings where trade unionist and managers are present prove difficult either because they evoke conflict or because they bury it.

There are also differences between members that have to do with their different positions in society. Parents, as parents, do not have the same organizational back-up as other representatives. They cannot get papers typed up and information researched. Their leverage on argument is based differently. It is reported that some parents tend to revert to other roles (as, for example, employers) in their participation in groups. They tend to withdraw from contentious discussion between more powerful institution-based representatives. As one teacher puts it, 'being a parent is a valid experience on which to draw, but few people recognize it'.

Other projects record similar observations about differences between members of community-linked groups. Apologists for Education Work Councils (**C1**) remark that, because of their lack of institutional back-up and visible base and because they voice their concerns in different terms, parents, trade unionists and students have found difficulty in achieving impact on some of these councils. They are reported to be among the groups most likely to drop out. In the Industry Project in Cleveland (**A4**) it is reported that industrial managers have resisted the recruitment to working parties of trades unionist, fearing propoganda. The report is made, however, by a manager who, with the benefit of experience, is regretting the resistance he once offered.

CONFLICT AND RESOLUTION

Where a diverse group of people have become visible to each other conflict will occur. Eventually, the findings of the research at 'Elin' (**F1**) suggest that young men and women are having difficulties adjusting to working life. An industrial manager, recruited after the group is first set up, disputes the findings hotly, causing some of the other members to wonder openly whether they have been overcritical of industry. Seizing on his authority as the only person from industry (which is true, the group has recruited no trade-union representative), the manager tables a paper. It minimizes the problems of transition, disputes the changing-world-of-work hypothesis, challenges the validity of all sociological research (although it quotes some of its own) and claims that the capitalist ethic, while not beyond criticism, 'is rather less severe in practice than on paper'. A differently argued, but similarly hot, attack on the proposals for curriculum development at 'Cloudly' School (**B1**) is mounted by one of the teachers. Middle-class whites, he contends, have no direct knowledge of what they study; they fail to penetrate the cultures of youngsters they seek to understand; youngsters understand the nature of reality of their neighbourhood very well and, in particular, they understand that it holds no joys for them; in any event, any curriculum proposal which emphasizes work in an inner city area is likely to prove a subtle form of indoctrination which, at best, will raise their hopes falsely. Strong stuff!

Such conflicts can prove expensive in terms of the group energy they absorb. The eventual recognition of conflict is unavoidable in any sustained relation between diverse members. It is what happens then that is important.

A *stand-off* is a withdrawal from fight: 'I'll stop shooting at you, if you'll stop shooting at me!' At 'Elin' (E1) the nervousness is about who is to be the target, first provoked by criticisms of employers, who are not at that time yet members of the group. It is expressed by teachers thinking they might also become targets. It is contained, for a while. But, after the paper presented by the industrial manager, there is no answer from the group and no further decisions for action are reported. Following the counter-rationale mounted by the 'Cloudly' (B1) teacher the employer representatives elect not to meet on school premises again. At Clydebank (D1) when the curriculum framework gives rise to criticism of the project from the grass roots, it is reported by the evaluators that teachers, heads and the project staff all tend to turn inwards on themselves and their own institutional concerns.

A *hijack* is a pre-emptive strike which is designed not so much to stop something, but to start something else. In the case of some of the Education Work Councils (C1) operations are reported to have been turned into a 'hurrahs for private enterprise', with all the pezaz of public relations events and presentation dinners. This is not what the originators of the idea had in mind. But there can be a tyranny of the articulate that benefits from a style and base for influence in which not everybody is practised.

Limitation of the expression of conflict is an option. For a time members of liaison groups in County Clare (F2) have doubts about whether the groups have the strength to contain and resolve their differences. A temporary consensus emerges for a softly softly (stand-off) approach. The sense of frustration grows. It is acknowledgement of this frustration that causes some of the groups to build into their agendas what they call limited gripe sessions. But most members stop short of looking at liaison groups as means of pressurizing any part of the system on behalf of only one part (hijacking). Progress, it is argued, 'is to be by consent, not leverage'.

Agreement to disagree occurs in 'Dane Park' School (E3). During the course of the workshops on syllabuses and materials different members of the team take quite different attitudes to how suitable it would be to admit unsavoury material into classrooms, such as material on prostitution or suicide. It is reported that they identify the differences, air them and agree that each teacher must take her or his own attitude to the issue.

Tolerance of the ambiguity of conflict raises a question about why it is possible in one place but not in another. One feature of the work at 'Dane Park' is reported as significant: it is that there has been a convention for discussion among school-based teams before the Careers Guidance Integration Project becomes involved. The project team comment to the head on what they call the self-mocking openness of the development teams. The head replies that it might have something to do with the fact that the staffing of the school is built on teaching teams which are expected to take part in their own forward-planning activity. The mutual visibility of participants is also recognized as important in reports of the Industry Project in Cleveland (A4), where differences of style, and even of value, become tolerable, even valued, in a group of people who have become visible thoroughly to each other (not as roles but as people). The provision of a cup of tea and a chance to chat before meetings may prove to be a significant part of the process. A similar observation is made in reports of Education Work Councils (C1), where the establishment of an early but manageable task is said to be as important for its process gains, of getting people into working relations with each other, as for any other gain it might make. The dilemma faced by the liaison groups in County Clare is that conflicts cannot be handled except where people know and trust each other; however, people cannot come to know and trust each other without risking conflict. In Cleveland the reports of movement to franker, more open discussion, are associated with opportunities for members of working parties to take part in weekend conferences and with the fact that friendships between teachers and adults-other-than-teachers develop (so that partners become people not labels).

ACTION

WHAT'S THE NEXT THING TO DO?

The chapter is summarized in this section and an application of an extension of the activity set out in Chapter 5 is detailed. Planning charts, all of which can be adapted and extended by planning groups engaged in the action, are laid out. However, these are not intended to be forms to be filled in; they are intended to be displays of the range of options which will confront most community-linked networks in the unfolding of their work.

WHAT?

Deciding on next action means knowing where we are now. In the planning chart shown in Figure 7.2 stages in the development of action are used as a basis for identification of next action. That each present achievement will indicate future work to be done is assumed. The consolidation of previous work makes a basis for subsequent action. There are provisions in the chart, on the left, for a description of what has been done and, on the right, for plans to consolidate that gain and use of it as a basis for future action.

WITH WHOM?

Entries on the right (Figure 7.2) will identify people and groups with whom to work. Among the people requiring attention at various points in the development of the franchise are: clients (people who are expected to gain from the action); users (people who are expected to implement the action); promoters (people who seek to catalyse the action); managers (people who can influence the feasibility and value of the action); audiences (people who have an interest in the action).

HOW?

Among the methods that are available are: informing (telling people things); canvassing

FIGURE 7.2   Planning what next?

Done [. . .]	To do [. . .]

Developing intentions
Do people know what is intended, why, in what settings and entailing what actions by whom?

Getting resources
Have all the people, places and materials been found, which can resource and inform the work sufficiently and with sufficient diversity?

Coordinating resources
Is what is being done sufficiently visible to members, so that gaps, overlaps and duplications can be identified, and to others, so that its existence and value is acknowledged?

Opening boundaries
Are people being put into new partnerships; is the diversity of assumptions and attitudes between partners acknowledged to the point where people can identify conflicts, and work them through to a stable resolution, without burning-up or burning-out?

Developing action
Is anything done that makes any useful difference to anything; is it action which clients can use and users can implement or, to the extent that is necessary, that audiences and managers can understand and support?

What else?

(testing and winning support); enquiring (asking for information); requesting (asking for help); reflecting (facilitating review and reactions); helping (offering material, consultancy, training).

This raises a number of options for next action. Who should be contacted in what way? The chart shown in Figure 7.3 maps possibilities for next action. No community-linked activity can afford indefinitely to ignore any of the groups or any of the methods.

BY WHOM?

The tasks identified by such a review are sufficiently diverse that it is inconceivable that responsibility for carrying it through can be left to one person or even a small number

FIGURE 7.3   Planning how?

	Clients	Users	Promoters	Managers	Audiences	Who else?
Inform						
Canvass						
Enquire of						
Request from						
Reflect with						
Help						
What else?						

of people. The review will identify the fact that different members of the network can carry out different parts of each next series of actions. Change is no single person's or group's sole responsibility.

SUMMARY AND CONCLUSION

The pre-vocational franchise supplements and realigns the apparatus and resources of schooling.

WHAT COUNTS AS VOCATIONAL IN THE PRE-VOCATIONAL CURRICULUM?

The realignment is for a closer correspondence between what people learn in schooling and what they do in adult working life. At the centre of that concern are intentions about the problems we want our young men and women to be able to solve and decisions we want them to be able to make; these are intentions for curriculum. At the centre of this book, in Chapter 4, is an argument for curricular intentions which identify and pursue students' motives: which means paying attention to their needs, attachments and interests.

The adult working life to which schooling is realigned is not concerned exclusively with paid employment in commerce and industry. Some projects, like the Community Newspaper Project (D3) are designed to raise awareness of enterprise undertaken in the leisure, cultural and political life of the community. Others, such as the Manningham Centre (C3), concern themselves both with the pursuit of conventional work and the creation of alternatives. Pre-vocational education is advocated as preparation for work both in paid employment and in alternatives to paid employment. These programmes make the possibility of multiple application explicit to clients.

In Chapter 4 is an invitation to action which no pre-vocational programme can avoid: the definition of curriculum intentions, the relation of existing activity to those intentions and the identification of needed further development.

FRANCHISE OR INTRUSION?

Pre-vocational education threatens intrusion on what was once called the 'secret garden of the curriculum'. Details of the nature of these intrusions are given in Chapter 3, where it leads to the identification of three franchises to enter and change. Later, in Chapter 6, a fourth franchise is identified.

The first franchise is modest, familiar anyway. It invites teachers to use their outside experience of adult working life in the development of curriculum as teachers-who-are-also-adults. The second franchise is less modest, inviting colleagues to share in the development and implementation of cross-curricular work in schooling. They will influence each other's work, losing exclusive concerns with aspects of curriculum. The third franchise invites entry by adults-other-than-teachers. It is linked closely to the notion of experience-based learning, elaborated in Chapter 6. But the experience base leads also to new learning by teachers and by adults-other-than-teachers, including people higher in the policy-making chain. Details of how the third franchise leads to gains by these learners-other-than-students appears in Chapter 1. The fourth franchise permits entry to the control of curriculum by students. It invites them to learn from each other and to influence what teachers do. It is elaborated in Chapter 6.

The progress of the pre-vocational franchise does not, invariably, run smooth. In Manningham Careers Centre (C3) it has entailed a radical shift from traditional roles, calling on skills and resilience which cannot be assumed to be an inevitable product of either the position or training of teachers or careers officers. The workers at Manningham accept the consequences because professional services should 'respond to client needs, rather than just telling them about the services they can have'. But it is unwise to assume such willingness to sully the purity of conventional practice. Realignments of practice are as likely to be evolutionary as revolutionary. Indeed, some which set out with radical intentions, such as the Clydebank EC Project (D1), find themselves settling for 'adjustments rather than big changes'. In some cases there has been outright and effective resistance by, for example, teachers at 'Cloudly' School (B1) who regard new curriculum proposals as inferior to what they already have in mind. The implication is that professional workers will need to be convinced as to why they should accept intrusion and why, in particular, they should change practice to take account of pre-vocational intentions (rather than the variety of other intentions which they, and others, can argue should be brought into curriculum).

REAPPLIED OR NEW CURRICULUM?

There are examples here of pre-vocational development which diversify existing curriculum by reapplying it to pre-vocational intentions. The use made of work shadowing within an existing music-department programme (A1) is an example. There are also examples of the production of additional curriculum requiring new time, like the fourth- and fifth-year social-education syllabuses produced at 'Dane Park' School (F3). A theoretical argument, mounted in Chapter 3, suggests that the reapplication of existing curriculum material is at least as likely to improve students' life chances as the development of new curriculum, that it is feasible, in the sense that there is no part of existing curriculum which cannot be so reapplied, and that it is more likely to be recognized by professional workers as a viable base of operations.

TOPS-DOWN AND BOTTOMS-UP?

In no case has action been accomplished wholly on the basis of a 'top-down' initiative, not in the sense of something imported from outside the organization or something handed down by 'bosses'. Indeed some, like the Working Lives Project (A7), are grass-rooted schemes entirely and some, like the Community Newspaper Project (D3), are maintained against initial resistance from the hierarchy. Outside consultancy may be accepted, as it is in 'Dane Park' (F3), but the acceptance is based on the finding of common ground between concerns expressed inside the organization and intentions expressed by the 'outsiders'.

Handed-down pressure and support for pre-vocational education, in the forms of credentialization and money for action, may be accepted but are not necessary bases for action and are unlikely to prove sufficient as such. The two projects that have a national network with centrally conceived aims are the School Curriculum Industry Project (A4) and the Transition to Working Life Project (A3). In neither case do the central teams seek to exert control at the point of delivery. Neither, as a matter of fact, do the promoters of Technical and Vocational Education Initiatives and the Certificate of Pre-vocational Education. A central piece of Industry Project rhetoric is 'no prescription, no package'.

COORDINATOR OR COORDINATING TEAM?

In all cases, now including CPVE and TVEI schemes, the role of the local coordinator or coordinating team proves critical. Styles of coordinating influence are described in Chapter 4; stages of coordinating development are described in Chapter 7. In Chapter 4 is a suggestion that coordination is in a process of ecological exchange with the people who will implement the action. A repertoire of styles is described in which negotiation through the offer of new resources, consultancy which draws on user's experience and the generation of new knowledge about the situation will all form a part.

In Chapter 7 the tasks of coordination are outlined, identified as a matter of timing action to respond to the development of experience in the network. The use of a variety of methods, ranging from informing to reviewing, with a variety of groups ranging from users to audiences are described also. It is a demanding role. It is not surprising to find that the Industry Project (A4) and the Transition to Working Life Project (A3) establish local coordination at both the neighbourhood and institutional levels. Where no such coordinator exists, in smaller-scale projects like the Community Contacts Directory (C2), then the teachers who want to see the action undertaken must adopt the role of coordinator themselves.

ADOPTION, ADAPTATION OR CREATION?

The consequence is that pre-vocational education will be implemented differently in every different place. In Chapter 2 is an analysis of how innovation occurs by identifying helps and hindrances to change. A suggestion is that readiness for change can range between 'enthusiastic welcome' to 'outright rejection'; indeed, it can range beyond that to 'backlash'. The indicators to readiness are to be found in the organization's context and climate, the terms in which a proposal is put forward, the styles adopted by the promoters, the position of the users, the reaction of students and chance. There are enough possibilities for variation in readiness for change to guarantee that no proposal for action can be transferred from one situation to another without being adapted. The unforeseen, and the opportunities it offers for local and creative response, are illustrated by the, initially unplanned, establishment of liaison groups in County Clare (F2).

FORMS OF NETWORKING?

In all cases cited here the action has been undertaken in partnership with adults-other-than-teachers, a phrase coined by the Industry Project, but an idea common to all the projects. In Chapter 1 some of the variety of roles which the notion of adults-other-than-teacher can entail are outlined. They can reach beyond 'guest' roles to 'host' roles, exerting influence on schooling at design and implementation stages and in its political context. The resulting networking links are analysed in Chapter 3.

'Rooted' networks remain attached strongly to their host institution, operating from inside its bureaucracy to support their activity. The Community Contacts Directory (C2) is an example and so are the more radical activities of City-as-school (A2) and Brinnington Community High School (A6).

'Emergent' networks establish new organizational structures which cut across the boundaries of existing institutions. The Manningham Centre (C3) is attached to the careers service, but it also has roots in the community it seeks to serve, and those roots influence its activity. The Transition to Working Life Project (A3) establishes a steering group, with its own resources and procedures drawing on contributions from both inside and outside the institution with which it is working. The Liaison Groups in County Clare (F2) are 'hosted' strongly by the schools to which they are linked in their early days, but a great deal of what happens in County Clare is unforeseen in the early days and, among the developments encouraged by the host institution, is the establishment of liaison groups with some independence of the host.

'Free-standing' networks are the design feature of Education Work Councils (C1), having their own budgets, procedures and, in some cases, full-time personnel. But there are suggestions that these councils can themselves become bureaucratized, perhaps because some element of bureaucratic structuring of purpose and resources is necessary somewhere.

In Chapter 3 is a suggestion that a celebration of networks, without their dependence on bureaucracies acknowledged, would be naive. Indeed, most organizations have elements of both networking and bureaucracy in them. This is, in part, because bureaucracies represent a stable base of operations offering a degree of predictability and security to participants.

Much therefore depends on how much admission adults-other-than-teachers are offered to the 'host' roles. In Chapter 7 is a suggestion that parents, students and trades unionists may experience more difficulty in influencing the direction of activity because they do not have the same access to bureaucratic resources with which to support their participation.

POLITICS IN PRE-VOCATIONAL EDUCATION?

Pre-vocational education further politicizes schooling. This book is not intended to reverse that trend. Curriculum is an instrument of policy. Governments which make offers of resources to schooling which are conditional on the pursuit of policy-determined objectives acknowledge that reality. But they must not be surprised if a political response is developed to a political initiative. The proposal for Post-Youth Training Scheme Partnerships (**A5**) is concerned explicitly with taking and promoting a local view of what central government is doing.

No teacher involved in the pre-vocational franchise can avoid the fact that he or she is working a political scenario in a political theatre. Enfranchisement is power. Adults-other-than-teachers will take their own view of what is being proposed; they are supposed to do so.

The pre-vocational teacher is therefore working with a social system which is different from that in the classroom or the interview. It is a system with more capacity to diversify intentions, provoke conflicts, resist influence, develop caucuses and appeal to constituencies. The position and training provided for teachers and careers officers does not equip them for the demands of the new roles. Much of what are called the 'finesse', 'diplomacy' and 'bite' of the coordinator is offered from the goodwill, and personal resources and resilience, of professional people whose professionalism extends beyond the scripted, trained and mandated role.

LIMITS TO FRANCHISE?

Speaking of the pre-vocational franchise raises the question 'is there anything which cannot be franchised?'. What is there left for the teacher to do? The key answer to the question is in relation to what teachers do with students. That role is suggested in Chapter 6. There attention is paid to the way in which students are helped to anticipate, log, review and negotiate from what they learn elsewhere in franchised activity. In that chapter it is suggested that these tasks are variants on the best teaching question ever invented : 'how are you getting on with that?'. All the apparatus of managing learning (recording learning, participative and experiential methods, student-centred reviewing, the negotiation of learning objectives, counselling, reviewing outcomes and monitoring impact) are implicit in that question. Nobody is in a better position to do the work than professional educators. In a good many cases they were using its skills long before pre-vocational education became a bandwagon.

APPENDIX

SETTING-DOWN EXPERIENCE-BASED LEARNING

In this section more detail of formats and procedures designed to help students say and set down what they learn from experience-based programmes, such as work-experience programmes, is given. There are four sections representing a sequence of learning activity: preparation, logging, reviewing and negotiating.

E1 Preparing for experience-based learning
E2 Logging experience-based learning
E3 Reviewing experience-based learning
E4 Planning and negotiating from an experience base

E1 Preparing for Experience-based Learning

Among the variety of cues and questions about anticipations of work experience and similar placements are the following:

(a) what kind of placement do you want?
(b) it's different out there!
(c) write an application
(d) be ready!
(e) watch out!
(f) what do you want to gain?

(a) *What kind of placement do you want?*

Information is sought to help in decisions about who receives which placement.

> This form is designed to help us find you a suitable work experience placement. It is therefore important that you fill it in carefully by ticking one box next to each

question. It is not possible to choose a particular type of job, but we will do our best to place you in a job which matches your interests.

How do you feel about	LIKE	DON'T MIND	DISLIKE
1 Working indoors?			
2 Working outdoors?			
3 Working in a large organization?			
19 Dealing with the public?			
20 A job involving a long journey to work?			
What sort of work are you interested in at the moment?			

Source: Jamieson *et al.*, 1986 (from Wandsworth Industry Schools Project).

(b) *It's different out there!*

Some invite students to consider the ways in which norms and rules in the experience are going to be different from what they (may) have been used to; some of these statements border on exhortations to 'behave yourself', others invite students to express their own opinions and concerns about the differences.

Derwent Hill (Residential Centre) — Expectations

Name: Date:

Please underline the words that best describe any worries you may have about going to Derwent Hill.

Food   Getting on with staff
                                        from your school
Mixing with other   Working as   Getting lost
adults and staff   a team
            Getting on with   Missing friends
        pupils from other schools   and family
Working alone   Learning new skills   Being hungry
        Doing things that look   Clothes
            frightening
Putting yourself   Getting wet   Not being fit
    at risk   enough

Making important
decisions

Not knowing
what to do

Finding an activity
very difficult

Being tired

Your
appearance

Getting on with
pupils from your school

Not being warm
enough

Relationships with the
opposite sex

Smoking

Not being able
to sleep at night

Being sick on
the bus

Missing the bus

Not having the right
equipment

Source: TVEI Support Team, Sunderland, 1985.

(c) *Write an application*

Students are invited to apply for a placement, in much the same terms as in an application for a job.

(d) *Be ready!*

Some designs take students through a consideration of what they need to do to show up in good shape, in most cases to be on time and ready for the workplace, in this case to be ready to learn from the experience.

Project Assessment

It is expected that your project will involve:
1 a very high level of attendance
2 a strong commitment to:
   (a) organizing and identifying your role in the group
   (b) carrying out your role in the group
   (c) supporting/assisting others in the group with their tasks
3 a willingness to evaluate your own performance (self evaluation) and to comment on the performance of your group (group report)
4 an absolute effort to meet negotiated deadlines for completion.

Source: White (Victorian Institute of Secondary Education), 1984.

(e) *Watch out!*

Some procedures take students through an anticipation of physical dangers that the placement might entail, usually by getting them to think about what they are going to do to avoid various dangers, frequently represented by pictures and graphics on the material.

(f) *What do you want to gain?*

Some designs invite students to anticipate what it will be like, and to think about what they would like to get from the experience, in some cases leading to the writing of a contract with the teacher.

Work experience and you

This booklet has been written to help you get the best out of your work experience.

First, it helps you prepare for work experience (pages 4–12).

Next, it helps you find out about work while you are in a work-experience job (pages 13–26).

Then it helps you think about work [. . .] and about your future (pages 27–38).

You have a chance to go on work experience.

What will it be like? What is in it for you? How do you feel about going? What do you want to find out?

Write down your thoughts, the questions you'd like to ask, your hopes.

Source: Strathclyde Education Department (1980b).

E2   Logging Experience-based Learning

Much of the material developed to invite students to set down their learning is designed to be used as a kind of log; to be set down while the experience is still occurring. Material for logging experience-based learning experience, include the following cues and questions:

(a) how did you get on in your interview?
(b) make a job study
(c) think about the premises
(d) what hardware is used?
(e) think about the organization?
(f) how safe is it?
(g) what are unions for?
(h) how is the outfit doing?
(i) what are they looking for in their workers?
(j) would you need training?
(k) what differences between school and the workplace do you notice?
(l) are you enjoying it?
(m) how was it today?

(a)   *How did you get on in your interview?*

Where students had an interview before they embarked on their placement they can be helped usefully to reflect on what happened.

Your Interview

Give the name and job title of the member of the company's staff who first interview-ed you, such as Mrs   (personnel manager). Write briefly about the kinds of questions you were asked and the answers you gave.

After interviews, most people think of better answers and wish they had thought of them at the time. If this happened to you, write down what you think would have been better answers.

Source: Lawson, 1984.

(b)   *Make a job study*

Students are encouraged to interview workers, much as a researcher would.

Job Interviews

When you ask questions, try to follow these simple but important rules:

1   don't ask people when they are busy or when you are supposed to be working
2   take a notebook and jot down their replies in it
3   be polite, do not ask personal questions, and always thank people at the end of an interview.

The best way to interview people is for you to think up your questions beforehand. Then write down the questions at the top of a separate sheet or page in your notebook, leaving plenty of space for their replies.

Here are some questions which should help you to get started.

The job

1   What is the name of your trade or job?
2   What do you do in your job?
3   How long have you been doing this job?
4   Was there a training period? If so, how long did it last?
5   Did you attend any college courses? (give details)
6   Do you belong to a trade union?
7   What is the name of the trade union?
8   Can you move on to another kind of job? If so, what is it?

---

9   Can you be promoted? If so, to what job?

10   What advice would you give to a young person who is coming into this kind of work or who is thinking of taking it up as a career?

Source: Jamieson, 1984.

(c)   *Think about the premises*

Some procedures seek information, drawings and maps about the workplace and its location, its 'feel' and its facilities, in some cases inviting students to reflect on the meanings of the location of the workplace and the allocation of space within it.

Day One — And What a Day!

Organization

What time did you have to leave home to get to work?

What sort of transport did you use?

Did you have any difficulties in getting to work?

What sort of canteen facilities are available at the firm or nearby?

What breaks are you allowed during the day? Is it enough?

What sort of facilities are available for the staff? (e.g. washrooms)

Do you think they were satisfactory?

(Comments)

Do the rest of the staff make full use of them? How many people do you work with in this job? Who gives you your instructions?

Is the job likely to take you out of the premises?

Are you likely to have much contact with the general public? (Give details — e.g. in person, by phone, etc.)

Source: Education Department of Western Australia, 1982.

The Company's Premises and Employees

How large (in square metres) is the place where you work?

How many floors does the company occupy?

List all the main departments in the company.

> Which two departments take up the greatest amount of space? Why do they need so much space?

Source: Lawson, 1984.

(d) *What hardware is used?*

Students are invited to look out for the tools, equipment, machines and other hardware used and, in some cases, to enquire into consequences for people's working lives.

New Technology

These questions need only be answered if they are relevant to your organization. Ask a helpful employee to help you answer these questions if they have time.

The place you are working in may or may not have machinery to do certain jobs. If it has, how old approximately are the machines?

Has the sort of work changed over the last 5 years because of the introduction of new machines? This would include the use of video in schools, new cash registers in shops, etc.

Has the introduction of any new machines/computers lost any jobs in the last 5 years? Or has it made work a lot easier?

In relation to new technology, how do the workers in your organization see the future of their company, and how do they feel it will affect the type of jobs they are doing.

Source: Brass (undated).

(e) *Think about the organization*

Some designs invite portrayals of the organization: its size, workforce, management, ownership, customers, raw materials, processes, products, services, advertising and controls. Again, students are being asked to do research. But, in some cases the procedures invite students to reflect on the significance of some of the organizational features they find, to some extent anyway.

How many people are employed by the company? Full-time Part-time

Women
Men

Students working after school/college and/or at weekends

Total

There will probably be people of many different ethnic origins at your place of work. See if you can discover, by asking them, where they or their families originated. Make a list and, using an atlas, find out how far they travelled.

Source: Lawson, 1984.

(f)   *How safe is it?*

Some procedures invite students to consider safety, how it can be secured and what the workplace has to help secure it.

Day Two — So Much to Learn!

Safety and Workers' Compensation

What safety regulations does the firm have in regard to clothing, footwear and personal appearance?

Is there any sort of safety programme? (e.g. signs, posters, lectures, etc.)

What safety rules must you follow if using any equipment?

Do you think these rules were enough?

Were they followed by other employees?

What is workers' compensation?

Who pays for workers' compensation coverage?

If you were injured on the job, how would workers' compensation help you?

Does workers' compensation apply on every job?

Source: Education Department of Western Australia, 1982.

(g)   *What are unions for?*

Students are invited to enquire into union activity, relating it to the benefits that it may bring to workers.

4   Does the union help its members with

. . .	health and safety	. . .	basic pay
. . .	conditions at work	. . .	overtime piecework or bonus
. . .	training and apprenticeships	. . .	sickness benefit
. . .	re-training	. . .	industrial injuries and compensation
. . .	fringe benefits (e.g. holidays	. . .	redundancy
. . .	legal advice on employment	. . .	new technology

. . . disciplinary action		. . . productivity deals
. . . equal opportunities		. . . attracting new investment

5   How does the union work for its members?

Often	Sometimes	Never	
. . .	. . .	. . .	day-to-day contact on the shop floor
. . .	. . .	. . .	union branch meetings
. . .	. . .	. . .	recruiting new members
. . .	. . .	. . .	mass meetings
. . .	. . .	. . .	attendance at conferences, trades councils, etc.
. . .	. . .	. . .	consultation with the management
. . .	. . .	. . .	negotiations with the management
. . .	. . .	. . .	industrial action (go-slow, strikes, etc.)
. . .	. . .	. . .	meeting MPs or councillors

6   How can ordinary members take an active part in union affairs?

7   Why do people join trade unions?

Source: Brass (undated).

(h)   *How is the outfit doing?*

Some designs invite students to develop an account of how the workplace has developed and where it is likely to go from here.

> Write a short account of the history of the company, noting particularly important dates, developments, inventions, discoveries, the opening of new branches, etc. Try to collect pictures and draw diagrams where these will add to your account. The company may have published a booklet on its history, its growth and achievements and you could use this for reference. If you are allowed to keep it you can put it in your folder, but read it first and still put your own account here.

Source: Lawson, 1984.

(i)   *What are they looking for in their workers?*

Some procedures invite students to consider what sort of workers are sought in this workplace.

What Kind of Person is the Employer Looking For?

Employers are not interested in applicants who will not do a good job. No one is going to pay you if your work is a waste of money.

Which of these are the most important in this type of work?

- ☐ keenness to work
- ☐ keenness to train
- ☐ skills
- ☐ honesty
- ☐ personality

- ☐ ability to get on with the public
- ☐ ability to get on with workmates
- ☐ education, qualifications
- ☐ experience
- ☐ personal appearance, voice, manner

Would These Spoil Your Chances?

		Turned down	
ARE APPLICANTS REJECTED FOR THESE REASONS?		Sometimes	Quite often
SCHOOL	Poor reading, writing & spelling	. . . ☐	. . . ☐
PERFORMANCE	Poor arithmetic	. . . ☐	. . . ☐
	No 0 grades	. . . ☐	. . . ☐

Source: Strathclyde Education Department (1980b).

(j) *Would you need training?*

Students are invited to enquire into training requirements and provisions.

Training and Education

Training Does the firm or organization where you are working or training arrange for the education and training of its permanent employees? Is there training (tick). . .

on the job ☐   in a special training department ☐   in a workshop ☐
at a local FE or other kind of college ☐

Does the organization arrange for its employees to go on courses organized by industrial training boards?

Yes ☐   No ☐   If the answer is 'yes', which training board(s)?
Is the training . . .   over a year ☐   over more than a year ☐
on day release ☐   on one or two days in a year ☐
over a month or two in the early stages of employment ☐
on block release ☐

Do employees who go on these training programmes have . . .

day release or block release at a college ☐   full-time study ☐
part-time study at a college ☐   a degree course or
other (give details) ☐

Does the company or organization support YTS? . . . Yes ☐   No ☐

If so, what are the details of the scheme (write in)?:

(i)   Training;
(ii) Off-the-job at college or a centre;
(iii) Work experience;

Source: Jamieson, 1984.

(k)   *What differences between school and the workplace do you notice?*

Students are invited to report their experience in terms which identify responsibilities, relations, timings, dress, controls and language which may be different from what they find in schooling; in some cases procedures leave the students to identify any such differences in their own terms.

A New Language

You will be hearing lots of new words in your workplace which you have never heard before. List all the new words you hear below, and if you have time ask their meanings, or find out when you return to school.

WORDS   MEANING

Source: Brass (undated).

How is work different from school?

Source: Strathclyde Education Department (1980b).

(l)   *Are you enjoying it?*

Some procedures invite students to say what they like and do not like about being in the workplace.

TOPSHOP First Day

Tick the words that are true

On the first day I felt

Happy	☐	Excited	☐	Frightened	☐
Scared	☐	Lost	☐	Afraid	☐
Shy	☐	Confident	☐	Tired	☐
Wished I hadn't come		☐			

Source: Jamieson *et al.*, 1986 (from Coventry's TOPSHOP).

(m) *How was it today?*

Students are invited to make a day-to-day log, timesheet or diary. In some cases (including some cited above) different days in a diary are assigned to different focuses for attention.

Your Jobs

Don't forget to make notes of each new task you perform and remember to put a date next to each entry. Also add such things as:

- did you like or dislike doing it?
- do you think you performed the task very well, fairly well or badly?
- was your supervisor pleased with your work? What did he/she say about it?
- How would you feel about doing that particular job all the time, as a permanent occupation?

Explain your answer. You may think of other points to make about each task; if so, add them to the list above. Here, too, diagrams may be helpful.

Task performed   Date

Task performed   Date

Source: Lawson, 1984.

Dear Diary — Day Four (continued)

Being at work obviously involves DOING things. It also involves meeting and mixing with people.

Research and questions

(1) *A profile of my favourite workmate*
Name   Age (approx.)
Height   (approx.)   Length of service in firm

Qualifications for job
Specially admired qualities

(2)   Use this space to write a brief but detailed character study of the workmate you have chosen

---

Dear Diary — Day Five (continued)

Autographs and Best Wishes

Use this page to get your workmates to write a little note to you. Stick photos of them in if you wish.

Source: Jamieson *et al.*, 1986 (from Perryfields High School).

E3   Reviewing Experience-based Learning

Material for retrospectively reviewing experience, such as on work-experience programmes, includes the following cues and questions:

(a)   talk about it (loosely structured writing)
(b)   what happens?
(c)   what happened to you?
(d)   draw a picture of it (graphic representation)
(e)   what did it demand of you?
(f)   how did you feel?
(g)   talk about the people you met
(h)   what have people told you about yourself?
(i)   what have you learned?
(j)   did you learn what you set out to learn?
(k)   what was new about it?
(l)   how does your experience compare with other students?

(a)   *Talk about it*

Students are invited, in their own terms, to write essays, develop written scenarios or write reports of their experience.

Capturing the Experience of Work

Now try writing about your own experience of work in which you aim to:

● capture the personalities of the people with whom you work
● show what kind of relationship you have with them
● describe your thoughts and feelings about the job.

You could tackle this writing in a number of different ways:

a   *as a piece of autobiographical writing* in which you use the word 'I' and describe as truthfully, accurately and honestly as possible one or two memorable moments at work as they actually happened to you

b   *as a story* in which you invent fictional names for the characters (including yourself), but base the events on your own experience

c   *as a play*

d   *as a poem*

Choose from one of the following titles unless, of course, you can make up a better one of your own.

1   'A day in the life of a [. . .].'
2   'The day when everything seemed to go wrong.'
3   'The funniest thing that happened at work.'
4   'First day at work.'
5   'Learning the ropes.'
6   'I proved to myself I could do it.'
7   'People at work.'

Source: Jamieson *et al.*, 1986 (from William Gladstone High School).

(b)   *What happens?*

Some designs engage students in what is effectively a job study, writing in the third person and giving what appears to be 'objective' information; others combine observation and response.

Working For People

2   Does *this job* serve the people — individuals, the community —
    ☐   directly — you meet the people you serve. *Go on to 3A.*
    ☐   indirectly — you do not meet the public or customers — only workmates. *Go on to 3B.*

3A   *Jobs where you give a direct service* to customers, patients, children, the public, etc.

Who pays for this service? Customers? The government? The taxpayer?

Why do they pay for it? What makes this job valuable to the community or individuals?

What kind of person would be best for this sort of job? Does he/she need special skills, training, experience or personality?

3B   *Jobs where you give an indirect service* (you do not meet the public, customers, clients, etc.).

Find out why this job is important enough to the community for payment to be made. The employer pays wages — but where does he get the money from?

What makes this job valuable to the community?

4   How would you feel about a job working directly for people (customers, the public, patients, individuals, the community, etc.)?:

☐   it does not appeal to me much.
☐   it would appeal to me because.

Source: Strathclyde Education Department (1980b).

(c)   *What happened to you?*

Other designs invite specific descriptions of different aspects of events and actions in which the student is involved (although in some cases bordering on a job-study format).

(B)   *Your Observations and Impressions of Your Work Experience*
        Try to answer the following questions about your work experience

(1)   What job did you do and for how long were you doing the job?
(2)   How much training did you receive for your job?
(3)   Were the duties you were asked to do varied? List some of the duties.

Source: Jamieson *et al.*, 1986 (from Barnsley's SCIP-Trident programme).

(d)   *Draw a picture of it*

Some designs invite graphic representation of the places and event.

What is Noticed?

Choose the occasion you want to set down. Draw a map of where it happens showing the place, and any things and people that are there. Put yourself in.

Describe what you are doing here; say what you think you are doing best:

You could also write in 'bubbles' on the map:

●   anything about it you like and why

- anybody you admire and why
- anybody who tells you something important about yourself, what it is and how you feel about it.

Is anything said or done which is unexpected or which surprises you? What? Why?

Source: Law and Storey, 1986.

(e) *What did it demand of you?*

Some designs invite students to reflect on what the work demands in terms of skills, understanding, qualifications and other aspects of 'performance', although in some cases the information is asked for in terms which suggest an 'objective' job study and in others the student is asked to review what he or she was personally able to offer in response to job demands.

When you have completed your work experience period fill in the following report about yourself. Your employer will be completing an identical report. Try to work independently of your employer and then check your assessment with his.

	Good	Acceptable	Poor	COMMENTS
Attendance				
Time keeping				
Ability to understand written and spoken instructions				
Clear speech				
Adequate numeracy				
Ability to work without constant supervision				
Relationships with other employees				
Relationship with supervisor/manager				
Adaptability				

GENERAL COMMENTS

Source: Jamieson *et al.*, 1986 (from Perryfields High School).

(f) *How did you feel?*

Some designs invite expressions of pleasure and pain, some with more opportunity to elaborate personally the feelings than others.

First impressions are important, which did you feel like or think of your workplace during the first few hours on Monday?

Was the work you were doing interesting or was there anything you would have liked to change, i.e. perhaps you were not given enough practical things to do, or you were left for long periods.

What do you think was the best thing about this work experience?

Was there anything during the week which you were not happy about?

Are you glad you chose to do work experience?

Source: Brass (undated).

(g) *Talk about the people you met*

A few designs invite students to reflect on encounters with people specifically.

Your Friends at Work

Have you found that the people you work with are interested in your progress both during your training and at school/college? Do they ask questions about lessons and examinations, and make comparisons with their younger days? And do you like them to show an interest in your life out of work?

As you become more used to each other and get to know each other better, do you find that the people with whom you work become friendlier towards you and take more interest in you?

Will you go back to the company just to see the people there? Have you arranged to meet any of them during weekends or evenings in the future?

Source: Lawson, 1984.

Did anyone in the company mention the possibility of employment in future years?

Source: Brass (undated).

(h) *What have people told you about yourself?*

In some cases the review procedure includes an opportunity for people met on the experience to give their impressions of the student.

Personality
Where and When is this Based?

What is Noticed?

The words underlined describe the way you go about things in this situation:

calm		careful
decides for her/himself	does what is required of him/her	energetic
fair to others		fits in with others
friendly to others	gets things moving	hard working
makes his/her own plans	listens to others	mixes with others
open to suggestions from others		orderly worker
overcomes difficulties	pays attention to people's feelings	popular
seeks partners to work with		shows consideration for others
stands up to others	tireless	thorough
unruffled	works alone	

More detail about what you actually do in this situation goes here:

Observed by Whom?
Name(s)   Position(s)
Signature(s)   Date

Source: Law and Storey, 1986.

(i) *What have you learned?*

Students are invited to reflect on new learning, in terms of what they have been able to do, what they have learned to do, what information they have picked up, what traits and attitudes they have identified in themselves and what intentions for themselves they have identified. In one case cited impressions are sought from parents; the possibility of parents representing an important source of feedback to the student, or that the student and parents jointly make the resulting statement, is not ruled out.

Write down your honest opinion on what you feel you have learned on this work experience.

What are the main things you have learned about people and work during the week?

Source: Brass (undated).

Parent Report

1   Has this work experience programme been of benefit to your child? How?
2   In your opinion, how did your child react to the work experience programme?
3   What difficulties did your child experience?
4   Do you think that your child has been made more aware of choosing a career?

Source: Education Department of Western Australia (1980).

(j)   *Did you learn what you set out to learn?*

Some designs invite students to examine their experience in terms of objectives they set themselves at the beginning of the experience. Where students assess themselves it is, of course, a requirement that they have already had an opportunity to set themselves objectives.

Look back to page 4 where you wrote down things you wanted to find out. Now write down your answers:
1   The first thing I wanted to know was
     I have found out that
2   The second thing I wanted to know was
     I found out that

Source: Strathclyde Education Department (1980b).

(k)   *What was new about it?*

Much of the experience will be unanticipated. Some designs invite the expression of contrast with present experience.

Was there anything which was said or done which was a surprise to you?

How is work different from school?

Source: Brass (undated).

(1)   *How does your experience compare with other students?*

One design requires students to get into discussion with others to disclose and compare experiences and responses.

Share Your Work Experience

You can share your experience as a group, so that others can learn from your experience, and you can learn from theirs.

Before you begin:

- Check through your own report.
- Have you answered all the questions that apply to your work experience?
- Will the others be able to understand what you have written and your drawings, sketches, etc.?
- Do your answers give a clear picture of the, jobs you saw or did?

Your teacher will divide the class into small groups of 3–4 people. Make sure that in your group the others were at different types of work experience.

When the teacher tells you — or when the members of your own group are ready:

- Swap your reports. Read each others'.
- Makes notes on some paper about things you want to ask the writer of each report.

Comparing Your Experience

This page is for you, as a group, to explain how the work experience described in this booklet compares with the experience of other members of the group.

Here are the group's impressions of the jobs described in this booklet.

We thought working for   (Name of organization)
would be

We compared the jobs described in this booklet with the jobs seen or done by other members of the group.

We thought the good things about the experience described in this report are

and the things that were less satisfactory were

Signed (group leader)...   Date . . .

Source: Strathclyde Education Department (1980b).

E4   Planning and Negotiating from an Experience Base

Few designs incorporate material for entering a process of decisions and action as a consequence of an experience. Where they do they include the following cues and questions:

(a)   how do you rate the experience?
(b)   what does the experience suggest for your time at school or college?
(c)   how are your own plans shaping?

(a)   *How do you rate the experience?*

Students may be asked to say how useful the experience has been in terms which might help a person to know whether to call on the resource again and, if so, how it might be improved. There are hints in some of the items that students might be party to such negotiations.

> Did the manager and any supervisor ask you how you felt your work experience week had gone? If the answer is 'yes' what did you say, were you asked if there should have been any changes for future work experience?

Source: Brass (undated).

> 26   Have you any other comment to offer? Can you suggest any improvements to the scheme?

Source: Montgomery, 1983.

(b)   *What does the experience suggest for your time at school or college?*

Students are invited to consider what they are going to do about the experience as they return to school or college and what other students might gain from their own experience. In at least one case it raises questions about what sort of changes other people ought to be making to schooling to take account of what has been learned in the placement, hinting at the possibility that students, on the basis of their experience, might enter a process of curriculum negotiation.

> (13)   Was there anything which you did whilst on work experience which will be helpful now you have returned to school?
> (14)   How do you feel about returning to school now your work experience is over?
> (15)   What advice would you give to other young people going on work experience?

Source: Jamieson *et al.*, 1986 (from Barnsley's SCIP-Trident programme).

> What would you say to any pupil in the future who is thinking of going into your work experience place in future years?

Source: Brass (undated).

> 14 What skills which are needed at work do you think should be taught at school?

Source: Jamieson, 1984.

(c) *How are your own plans shaping?*

Some designs invite students to relate the experience to their own plans for the future.

> What new skills have you learned at work that you will be able to use at home, at school or college? Will these skills make it easier for you to obtain permanent employment when this period of training/work experience is finished? Do you think that you might be able to use these skills to do jobs for friends and neighbours and perhaps earn 'pocket money'? Here, too, sketches might be helpful.

> Having considered your answers to the previous questions, what advice would you give to a friend who is about to start his/her first period of training or work experience and is rather frightened or anxious about the prospect?
>
> If the opportunity were available, would you like to continue your work as a full-time permanent employee? Explain your answer. How has this time of training or work experience helped you to decide what kind of job you would like to do when you start on a permanent career? Has it, perhaps, caused you to think about continuing your education to gain higher qualifications? Or has it made you want to begin work and earning as soon as possible?

Source: Lawson, 1984.

> 6 Has the experience helped you to make up your mind about the type of work you would like to do on leaving school?

Source: Watts, 1983 (from Cleveland Education Authority).

> Has going on work experience helped you in your future career decision?

Would you like to work for your organization when you leave school?

Source: Brass (undated).

3 What do I need to do now to help me develop and gain from the experience of work that I have had?

Source: Jamieson *et al.*, 1986 (from Barnsley's SCIP-Trident programme).

REFERENCES

Armstrong, D., Bazalgette, J. and Reed, B. (1984) *Working With Your Own Resources*, The Grubb Institute, London.

Bates, I. (1983) Participatory teaching methods in theory and practice: the Schools Council 'Careers' Project in School, *British Journal of Guidance and Counselling*, Vol. 11, No. 2.

Bazalgette, J. (1978) *School Life and Work Life: a Study of Transition in an Inner City*, Hutchinson, London.

Bernstein, B. (1967) Open schools, open society, *New Society*, 14 September.

Bernstein, B. (1971) *On the Classification and Framing of Educational Knowledge*. In M. F. D. Young (Ed.) Knowledge and Control, London: Collier-Macmillan, London.

Blakey, K. (1984) Hair!, *Times Educational Supplement*, 2 November.

Brass, M. (undated) *Work Experience in Newham Schools*, Newham Education Authority, Newham.

Bray, E. (1982) *Work Experience in Clydebank*, Strathclyde Department of Education, Dunbarton.

Bronfenbrenner, U. (1979) *The Ecology of Human Development*, Cambridge University Press, Cambridge.

Callan, J. and Gleeson, J. (undated) *Local Liaison Groups*, SPIRAL Curriculum Development Centre, Shannon.

Canon, M. J. (1979) *Experience-based Learning: a Formative Evaluation Report*, SPIRAL Curriculum Development Centre, Shannon.

Dahrendorf, R. (1979) *Life Chances*, Weidenfeld and Nicolson, London.

Davies, J. P. (1981) *The SITE Project in Northampton 1978–80*, Nene College, Northampton.

Daws, P. (1968) *A Good Start in Life*, Careers Research and Advisory Centre, Cambridge.

Daws, P. (1977) Are careers education programmes in secondary schools a waste of time?, *British Journal of Guidance and Counselling*, Vol. 5, No. 1.

Education Department of Western Australia (1982) *Work Experience Diary*, WAED, Perth WA.

Elliott, J., Bridges, D., Ebbuts, D., Gibson, R. and Nias, J. (1981) *Cambridge Accountability Project: a Summary Report*, Social Science Research Council, London.

European Community Action Programme (1980) *Thirty Pilot Projects*, EEC, Brussels.

Evans, K. and Law, B. (1984) *Careers Guidance Integration Project: Final Report*, NICEC, Hertford.

Fawcett, B. (1985) *What TRACE of Careers Education?*, Longman Resources Unit for the Schools Council, York.

Fletcher, C., Caron, M. and Williams, W. (1985) *Schools on Trial*, Open University Press, Milton Keynes.

Fullan, M. (1972) Overview of innovative process and the user, *Interchange*, Vol. 3, Nos. 2–3.

Fullan, M. (1985) Change processes and strategies at the local level, *Elementary School Journal*, Vol. 85, No. 3.

Fullan, M. and Pomfret, A. (1977) Research on curriculum instruction implementation, *Review of Educational Research*, Vol. 47, No. 1.

Fullan, M., Miles, M. B. and Taylor, G. (1981) *Organisation Development in Schools: the State of the Art*, National Institute of Education, Washington DC.

Furtherwick Park School (1985) *Pre-vocational Education 1985–86*, Furtherwick Park School, Canvey Island.

Giddens, A. (Ed.) (1972) *Emile Durkheim: Selected Writings*, Cambridge University Press, Cambridge.

Grubb Institute of Behavioural Studies (1982) *Report and Assessment of a Research and Action Project with Unemployed Young People, 1978–81*, Grubb Institute, London.

Handy, C. (1976) *Understanding Organisations*, Penguin, Harmondsworth.

Havelock, R. G. (1973) The Change Agent's Guide to Innovation in Education, *Educational Technology Publications*.

Holmes, S. and Jamieson, I. (1983) *Further Uses of 'Adults Other Than Teachers'*. In A. G. Watts (Ed.) Work Experience and Schools, Heinemann, London.

Holmes, S. and Lightfoot, M. (1981) The world in the classroom, *Times Educational Supplement*, 30 January.

Howden, L. (1985) About their needs, not our services, *NICEC Training and Development Bulletin*, No. 29.

Jamieson, A. (1984) *Work Experience and Industrial Visits*, Careers Research and Advisory Centre, Cambridge.

Jamieson, I. and Lightfoot, M. (1982) *Schools and Industry*, Methuen for the Schools Council.

Jamieson, I., Newman, R. and Peffers, J. (1986) *Work Experience Workbooks*, Longmans Resources Unit for the School Curriculum Development Committee.

Law, B. (1977a) System orientation: a dilemma for the role conceptualisation of secondary school counsellors, *British Journal of Guidance and Counselling*, Vol. 5, No. 2.

Law, B. (1977b) What do teachers learn from in-service guidance training?, *The Counsellor*, Vol. 2, No. 2.

Law, B. (1978) The concomitants of system orientation in secondary school counselling, *British Journal of Guidance and Counselling*, Vol. 6, No. 2.

Law, B. (1979) The contexts of system orientation in secondary school counselling, *British Journal of Guidance and Counselling*, Vol. 7, No. 2.

Law, B. (1981) Community interaction: a mid-range focus for theories of careers development in young adults, *British Journal of Guidance and Counselling*, Vol. 9, No. 2.

Law, B. (1982) *Beyond Schooling*, NICEC, Hertford.

Law, B. (1983) Working classes, *Education Section Review of the British Psychological Society*, Vol. 7, No. 2.

Law, B. (1984) *The Uses and Abuses of Profiling*, Harper and Row, London.

Law, B. (1985) Experience-based learning for teachers, *NICEC Training and Development Bulletin*, No. 28.

Law, B. and Roberts, C. (1983) On leading horses to water, *NICEC Training and Development Bulletin*, No. 24.

Law, B. and Storey, J. (1986) *Is it Working?* British Petroleum Educational Services, London.

Law, B. and Ward, R. (1981) *Is Career Development Motivated?*. In A. G. Watts, D. E. Super and J. M. Kidd (Eds.) Career Development In Britain, CRAC, Cambridge.

Law, B. and Watts, A. G. (1977) *School, Careers and Community*, Church Information Office, London.

Lawson, E. (1984) *Work Experience and Training Diary*, Careers Research and Advisory Centre, Cambridge.

Marsh, M. (1981) Some sort of dynamic process, *NICEC Training and Development Bulletin*, No. 19.

Marsh, M. (1982) *Guidance and Alternative Curriculum Perspectives*, Marjorie Marsh, Cleveland (mimeo).

Maslow, A. H. (1954) *Motivation and Personality*, Harper and Row, London.

McDonald, B. and Walker, R. (1976) *Changing the Curriculum*, Open Books, London.

McMahon, A. (1984) *Guidelines for Review and Internal Development in Schools: Secondary School Handbook*, Longman Resources Unit for the Schools Council, York.

Miles, M. B. (1967) *Some Properties of Schools as Social Systems*. In G. Watson (Ed.) Change in School Systems, National Training Laboratories, Washington DC.

Montgomery, R. (1983) *Work Experience: a School-Based Approach*. In A. G. Watts (Ed.) Work Experience in Schools, Heinemann, London.

Morrish, I. (1976) *Aspects of Educational Change*, George Allen and Unwin, London.

Poulter, I. and O'Connell, P. (1984) *Furtherwick Park School: a Survey of Staff Attitudes*, Furtherwick Park School, Canvey Island.

Reed, B. and Bazalgette, J. (1983) *TWL Network and Schools*. In A. G. Watts (Ed.) Work Experience and Schools, Heinemann, London.

Roe, A. (1956) *The Psychology of Occupations*, J. Wiley and Sons, New York.

Roberts, K. (1981) *The Sociology of Work Entry and Occupational Choice*. In A. G. Watts, D. E. Super and J. M. Kidd (Eds.) Career Development in Britain, Careers Research and Advisory Centre, Cambridge.

Roberts, C. and Law, B. (1985) *No Certain Place to Go?*, National Institute for Careers Education and Counselling, Hertford.

Rogers, C. (1965) *Client Centred Therapy*, Houghton Mifflin, Boston.

Rutter, M. (1979) *Fifteen Thousand Hours*, Open Books, London.

SPIRAL (1982) (Shannon Project of Interventions for Relevant Adolescent Learning) *A Communal Responsibility for All Our Young People*, SPIRAL Curriculum Development Centre, Shannon.

Stenhouse, L. (1975) *An Introduction to Curriculum Research and Development*, Heinemann, London.

Strathclyde Education Department (1980a) *EEC Project on the Transition from School to Working Life*, Strathclyde DE, Dunbarton.

Strathclyde Education Department (1980b) *EEC Project*, Strathclyde DE, Dunbarton.

Stronach, I. and Weir, A. D. (1983) *Once Upon a Timetable*, Jordanhill, College of Education, Glasgow.

Toogood, P. (1984) *The Head's Tale*, Dialogue Publications, Telford.

Tucker, S. (1985) *Post-YTS Initiatives*, Youthaid and the National Youth Bureau, London.

TVEI Support Team, Sunderland (1985) *Student Profiles and Records of Achievement*, Borough of Sunderland, Sunderland.

TWL Network Resources Centre (1982) TWL: the growth of an idea, *TWL Bulletin*, No. 1.

Watson, G. (1967) *Change in School Systems*, National Training Laboratories, Washington DC.

Watts, A. G. (1983) (Ed.) *Work Experience and Schools*, Heinemann, London.

Watts, A. G. (1983) *Education, Unemployment and the Future of Work*, Open University Press, Milton Keynes.

Watts, A. G. (1986) *Work Shadowing*, Longmans Resources Unit for the School Curriculum Development Committee, York.

White, P. (1984) Towards work-based assessment: further lessons from the youth action program, *Viewprints*, No. 2.

Wirtz, W. (1975) *The Boundless Resource*, New Republic Books, Washington DC.

Wragg, T. (1984) Personal, *Times Educational Supplement*, 1 June.

INDEX